Fairways to Heaven

One Shot at a Time...
By
Jon Decker

ReadersMagnet, LLC

Fairways to Heaven: One Shot at a Time...
Copyright © 2024 by Jon Decker

Published in the United States of America

Library of Congress Control Number: 2024909750
ISBN   Paperback: 979-8-89091-595-5
ISBN   Hardback: 979-8-89091-596-2
ISBN   eBook: 979-8-89091-597-9

The opinions expressed by the author are not necessarily those of ReadersMagnet, LLC.

ReadersMagnet, LLC
10620 Treena Street, Suite 230 | San Diego, California, 92131 USA
1.619. 354. 2643 | www.readersmagnet.com

Cover design by Ericka Obando
Interior design by Dorothy Lee

DEDICATION

This book is dedicated to Carla Sokol. Thank you for loving me unconditionally and supporting me through this writing journey. I love you dearly.

FOREWORD

Ted J. Odorico

Editor, *Golf Tips Magazine*

Over my 30-year golf career, I have met many interesting people both on and off the course, from everyday store clerks to Fortune 500 CEOs. No matter their background, they all have one thing in common — a tremendous love and respect for the game of golf. Several years ago, I decided to move to Florida to pursue my golfing career full time. While getting things organized, I began hosting a weekly podcast, *Golf Talk Live*. It was during the early years that I met Jon Decker. He had written his first book, *Golf Is My Life: Glorifying God Through the Game,* describing both his golf and spiritual journey. Jon learned of my podcast and decided to reach out as a fellow golf professional to offer his time as a guest to talk about his book. As a fellow Christian, the book piqued my interest, therefore I quickly added him to the schedule. We both share a true passion for the game as well as an enthusiastic relationship with God. It became very clear that this book was a personal life journey for Jon, a way back to his

Christian roots. Jon has become a regular guest on my show and, as a result, our friendship has continued to develop.

A few years ago, I purchased *Golf Tips Magazine* and quickly added Jon as one of the magazine's Top 25 Instructors. His knowledge and experience of the game have proven to be quite invaluable to our readers. During the time of the magazine's purchase, Jon expressed interest in producing a featured article for the publication titled *Fairways to Heaven*. It was certainly risky for any mainstream golf publication to have a faith-based article within its pages. This was something he strongly felt led to write, and as a fellow Christian I happily obliged. There was apprehension in the beginning as we were not certain how it would be received, being that not everyone shared our faith. We did experience a little negative feedback, but nothing compared to the overwhelming eagerness and support from the readers. Jon has put a great deal of thought and passion and carefully woven both golf and scripture into each article. It has become a staple inside the pages of the magazine and continues to receive positive reviews.

Fairways To Heaven has become another way for Jon to continue exploring his own personal and spiritual journey. Golf is merely a vessel he's chosen to help spread the Word. My hope is that through the pages of Jon's latest book you will find the courage and strength to find your own path. I'm confident that, as you turn the pages, you will find it an interesting and enlightening read.

Enjoy your journey!

Ted J. Odorico

Introduction and Acknowledgements

My Second Act…

"Oh, give thanks to the Lord, for He is good! For His mercy endures forever. Oh, give thanks to the God of gods! For His mercy endures forever. Oh, give thanks to the Lord of lords! For His mercy endures forever." (Psalm 136: 1-3)

There is something magical about listening to music late in the day, alone on the back of the driving range, with a small bucket of balls by your side. One by one, each well-struck shot produces a sound that entices the senses for just one more. However, with each shot there is a race against time, as the summer sun slowly leans toward the western horizon. Throughout my lifetime, I have found that when I listen to music while I practice, I no longer focus on my swing technique. My mind begins to clear of any technical garbage that may have been left over from my last practice session and my swing finds its natural beat. As the rhythm of my swing improves, suddenly everything falls into its proper place. My golf swing begins to flow, like Sunday morning maple syrup over hot pancakes, hours before church.

I have always loved the country/rock band the Eagles and found that, when I listened to the group's music while practicing or working around the house, my production improved. Songs like *Take it to the Limit, I Can't Tell You Why* and *New Kid in Town* are three of my favorites, but honestly, I love all the Eagles' work. The band grew in popularity during the 1970s until its breakup in 1980. After their breakup, *The Eagles Greatest Hits Album* was a constant sound on the radio, keeping the band relevant and far from forgotten by their millions of fans. Fourteen years after their breakup, in 1994, the band did the unthinkable: it reunited. Several years ago, I watched the two-part documentary *History of the Eagles: The Story of an American Band*. Don Henley, one of the cofounders of the group along with the late Glenn Frey, said during the interview when asked about the band reuniting, "I was okay with the notion of being in a band again. And maybe we could have the rarest of things in American life, which is a second act." For some reason, Henley's response resonated with me.

This book, *Fairways to Heaven: One Shot at a Time...*, is my second act. Typing those words in reference to my unexpected writing career is somewhat of a minor miracle, from my perspective. In January of 2012, I wintered in Hilton Head, South Carolina, to escape the bitter cold of Columbus, Ohio. One early morning, I sat at the kitchen table of my rental home and began writing my first book, *Golf Is My Life: Glorifying God Through the Game*. The writing process took four years to complete before the book was published in October of 2016.

Reluctantly, I took on that writing project knowing that I was going to need assistance with such a massive undertaking. So, I reached out to my longtime friend, former student and former senior writer for *Golf Digest*, Pete McDaniel. Pete is an award-winning author and former writer for Tiger Woods. He agreed to edit my work as well as provide a first-time author with a crash course in Writing 101. Pete's mentorship as well as his friendship was the earthly help I needed. God directed Pete McDaniel into my life for a reason and, without his help, my first book would have never been published.

Several days after the book was released, I received a phone call from my college roommate Jeff Davis. He eagerly opened the conversation by saying, "Jon, I ordered your book online and read it in two days." I replied, "Wow, Jeff that's awesome! If you had studied like that when we were at ECU (East Carolina University) you wouldn't have taken five years to graduate!" We both started laughing because he knew it took me five years as well. Jeff said, "I also ordered another book for my pastor, and we are going to start a Bible study along with your book." I replied to Jeff, "What a great idea!" That single conversation days after the book's release was the inspiration I needed and led to the creation of a Bible study. Over the next eight months, I traveled across eight states promoting the book and started 13 Bible studies along the way.

The marketing for the book started with a few speaking engagements and book signings, but soon led to radio and podcast interviews, newspaper articles and an interview and feature from my hometown television station, WLOS in Asheville, North Carolina. Social media was also very important in the marketing of the book and, through it, I met two people who were both instrumental in the creation of my second act, *Fairways to Heaven: One Shot at a Time…*

The first person I met was Dr. Angelica Napolitano (aka "The Golf Doc"). Angel, as she is commonly referred to by her friends, is a doctor of physical therapy from Jupiter, Florida. We connected through social media after she watched several of my instructional videos and later interviewed me on her podcast after reading my book. Several weeks after she received the book, she contacted me with an interesting observation. Although I was residing in Ohio and she in Florida, Angel realized that we had both lived in my hometown of Black Mountain, North Carolina, at different times of our lives. In fact, the homes we lived in were just over a mile from each other, proving to me that God does work in mysterious ways. One day while talking on the phone, she mentioned the phrase "Fairways to Heaven." When I heard it, I knew immediately that it would make a great title for a book and that if I ever decided to write another book, *Fairways to Heaven* would be the title. Thank you, Angelica, for allowing me to use your idea for the title of this book. You are an Angel indeed!

The second was Ted Odorico. Ted hosts two podcasts, *The Women of Golf* and *Golf Talk Live*. Each two-hour *Golf Talk Live* episode includes a one-hour feature called *The Coaches Corner* followed by a special guest interview. Soon after my first book's release, I reached out to Ted to ask if I could be a guest on his show to promote the book. Ted was very accommodating and the interview went well. After the interview, Ted invited me to be a regular panel guest once a month on *The Coaches Corner*. Over time, we became great friends and one day he reached out to me with some exciting news. He was considering purchasing *Golf*

Tips Magazine and wanted to know what I thought. My response, "Ted, what an amazing opportunity!"

Once *Golf Tips Magazine* was purchased, Ted asked if I was interested in being a senior editor for the magazine, contributing instructional articles along with instructional videos. I was honored and said "Yes" to the wonderful opportunity. However, I did have a question for Ted but was somewhat hesitant to ask. "Ted, I would like to write a feature for the magazine that is Christian-based. The feature would be called *Fairways to Heaven.* The feature would start with scripture, tell a golf story as well as a life experience and show how Christianity, golf and life are all related. Would you allow me to write it?" Ted thought about it and gave me the response I was praying for; his response was "Yes."

Ted and I both knew that adding a Christian feature with scripture to a mainstream golf magazine was risky. After all, *Golf Tips Magazine* has been in publication since 1988. I said upfront, "Ted, you may get some pushback from some, but I really think that most of the readers will enjoy the feature." As predicted, there were a few who disapproved, but overall, the positive emails and responses received more than outweighed the negative, giving Ted and me the confidence to continue forward. The writing of *Fairways to Heaven* is what inspired this book. This book is a compilation of those columns from *Golf Tips Magazine.* Thank you, Ted, for having the courage to give *Fairways to Heaven* the platform it needed to reach the world.

During my lifetime, I have been blessed to have many people who have shaped my life, both personally and professionally, so I wanted to include some of them in the book. Throughout the book, there are several forewords called *As Seen Through My Eyes* that provide a personal entry into the chapter from their perspective. Also included in the book is a tribute to Phil Rodgers with personal testimonies titled *My Memories of Phil...* from my former coworkers from Grand Cypress. I would like to thank the following people who took the time to contribute to this book: Carl Alexander, Jason Bell, Eric Eshleman, Fred Griffin,

Joey Hidock, Blake Holbrook, Gus Holbrook, Lee Houtteman, Doug Lowen, Kraig Kann, Clark Kellogg, Dr. Ralph Mann, Kevin McKinney, Todd Meena, Dr. Matt Mingione, Dr. Angelica Napolitano, Ted J. Odorico, Brenda Pfeifer, Adrian Stills, Kevin Weeks, Harold Wyatt and Harry Zimmerman.

I would also like to thank Bill Studenc for all his help with the editing of this book and Jean Perpillant for the cover photograph. It was a pleasure working with you both.

Thank you to Jeremy Craft, director of golf operations at the Evermore Resort (formerly Grand Cypress Resort) in Orlando, Florida, for allowing me to shoot the cover for the book on the Links Course (formerly the New Course).

A special thank you to Dr. David Jeremiah and *The Jeremiah Study Bible*. This study Bible has been invaluable in helping me better understand the Word of God and how to apply it to this book.

The subtitle for the book, *One Shot at a Time,* is followed by three periods, also known as an ellipsis. An ellipsis is used in writing to show that something has been left out. First, my favorite number is three, so the first time I ever saw an ellipsis, the three periods immediately caught my eye. Second, since rededicating my life to Jesus Christ, every time I type an ellipsis, I say to myself: Father, Son and Holy Spirit. The symbolism of the ellipses is like the stamp placed on the envelope for my writing that is necessary for the message to be delivered. Without the Father, Son and Holy Spirit, my writing would be void of any structure or meaning. Finally, when I see the ellipses, I think of three golf balls and the repetitive nature of life and golf. Hit the first shot, find the ball, hit the second shot, and find the ball until the ball is finally holed out. This sequence of one shot at a time is the essence for the game of golf.

Every day of our life is like a single shot on the course that must be played, repetitively, one day at a time. Some days our life finds the fairways and others the deep rough, some life moments we want to remember, while others we try and forget. The key to our success on the course and in our life is often measured by our attitude. It is easy to have a good attitude when our ball has found the fairways of life, but, oh, how our attitude changes when we find the water after an errant tee shot. To lift my soul and improve my attitude during the low points of my life, I often listen to contemporary Christian music. I am amazed how music, especially music that praises the Lord, lifts my soul. Many of the old church hymns and contemporary songs that are popular today were inspired by the Psalms.

The Psalms are simply poetry, inspired by God. They can be read quietly, while sitting in a field alone under a shaded tree with the Lord or sung together in unison by a small group of believers. Like the sound of a beautiful refrain sung by a Sunday morning church choir, the intent of the Psalms is to praise God. Many of the Psalms were written by David during times of anguish and some during times of thanksgiving, while other were written by unknown authors whose intent was to glorify God. Like all scripture, reading the Psalms sets the tone for my daily life. Its melody reaches more than the human mind; it connects my soul with the Lord. By simply reading ***Psalm 136: 1, "Oh, give thanks to the Lord, for He is good! For His mercy endures forever,"*** I begin to feel an inner peace. However, this experience is magnified, as I read or sing the same verse out loud repeatedly. Suddenly, the darkness that once surrounded my life disappears. Just as the songs from the Eagles cleared my conscious mind while practicing alone and removed the skeletons that hid in the recesses of my mind, the reading of the Psalms is music to my ears.

As Seen Through My Eyes

by

Dr. Angelica Napolitano

Doctor of Physical Therapy, Jupiter, Florida

Black Mountain, North Carolina, is a small town with a historical golf course that was once home to the "World's Longest Hole." The front nine was designed by Donald Ross in 1929, and the back nine was added by course architect Joseph Holmes and golf professional and greenskeeper Ross Taylor in 1962. The signature hole on the back nine features a par-6 that measures 747 yards from the tips. But this is not the only thing that makes Black Mountain so special. Home to the late Reverend Billy Graham, Super Bowl Champion Brad Johnson and former NBA player Brad Daugherty, Black Mountain is known for its breathtaking mountainous views and a downtown area with a vintage vibe. As a young girl, I spent most of my summer and winter breaks visiting my father on Crestview Drive, a street just northwest of the golf course. A lot of my childhood memories and experiences were made there.

The grand opening of the back nine of the Black Mountain Golf Course in 1962. (Left to Right) Billy Joe Patton, runner-up 1954 Masters; Howard "Big Noise" Garland, financed the purchase of the property; Ross Taylor, PGA professional for the Black Mountain Golf Course; Clyde Small (friend of Billy Joe Patton) and the Reverend Bill Graham. Rev. Graham was instrumental in helping negotiate the purchase of the land, citing the importance of the golf course for the town of Black Mountain. Photo courtesy of Richard Hudson.

Fast forward 25 years later when I first met Jon and was living in Jupiter, Florida. We bonded over our discussions of golf and our respective professions within the industry. As an instructor, he had a deep history within the community, and I admired that about him. I was a young physical therapist who just began my journey as a practice-owner trying to brand myself as the "Golf Doc," so I felt privileged that Jon gave me guidance over the phone about the nuances of the game.

One day, I received a book in the mail titled *Golf is My Life: Glorifying God Through the Game*, written and personally autographed by Jon. We had talked about his book many times, but now I finally got to read it. I was excited! With my busy schedule, it took me longer to complete than I'd like to admit, but the book was captivating. I knew that Jon was a Christian, but I learned a lot more about his faith and how it guided him throughout his life, teaching him how to turn his dreams into a reality, even in the face of adversity.

I was overwhelmed with gratitude with our new friendship, but I felt like I didn't deserve it. Why would someone who has worked with some of the world's greatest athletes and stood so firmly in his beliefs take time out of his day to talk with me? I didn't have a strong faith or even come close to Jon's success. This was my first experience with imposter syndrome, and it was purely out of respect and admiration for someone else. But that is just Jon, the nicest guy who would do just about anything for anyone. He really is a strong Christian man at heart who puts God first above all else. I am proud of his accomplishments and proud to be his friend.

Another interesting discovery I made while reading his book ties back to my childhood, a fact neither of us knew from each other's past, yet it played such a pivotal role in our lives. Once again, I was overwhelmed with emotions, but this time they were nostalgic. Jon and I both grew up in the same town, Black Mountain. A town so small that most people don't even know it exists. After my discovery, I immediately called Jon. I couldn't believe it! How did we not know this about each other? The house Jon grew up in was but a mile from my father's house – we were so close yet so far. We talked about our childhoods and how we would go sledding after a big snow from Homer's Chapel, a small church located on a mountainous hill, down the steep incline and onto the frozen golf course. We talked about Lake Tomahawk, the golf course, the town, everything. We had so many memories in common, only they were many years apart. Up until this time, very few people, other than my family, could relate to these experiences, which now mean even more to me since my dad has passed away. Black Mountain is a place that holds a lot of sentimental value to me and a time in my life that I will never forget.

Not long after I finished reading his book, I mentioned to Jon that I made T-shirts with my logo on them to promote my business. The design was simple, so I wanted something catchy on the back. I thought with my name being Angel that "Fairways to Heaven" sounded appropriate. When I told Jon, he agreed, and that was the end of our conversation. I didn't know how much this T-shirt slogan meant to Jon until one day when he asked for my permission to use it as the title of his next book. Without hesitation, my answer was yes! Of course, he could use it; in fact, I was honored and would love nothing more. The story of how the title of this book came to be was certainly directed by God, and I'm so flattered to be a part of it. Looking back at how our friendship has evolved, I am now reminded that not only is the world a small place, but that God puts certain people in your life for a reason, and for that I am eternally grateful.

Chapter 1

1980:
The Birth of a Dream

"For it is not you who speak, but the spirit of your father speaking through you." (Matthew 10:20)

My life began in Augusta, Georgia, in January of 1967, not far from arguably the most famous golf venue in the world, Augusta National Golf Club. I guess you could say that golf is in my blood. I was born at Fort Gordon Army Base but only lived in Augusta six months before my father was stationed in Landstuhl, Germany. My earliest memories of life are from the early 1970s living in Bryson City, a small, quaint town nestled in the Smoky Mountains of Western North Carolina. Our family had moved there after my father's military service was complete. My childhood was like growing up in a cocoon. I felt loved and safe, and I knew all my neighbors. Bryson City may have been sleepy, but I sure wasn't! I was a forward-thinker, always dreaming of where I was going to go and what I was going to do with my life.

My first dream was to be a garbage man. I loved the sound of the big truck as it came rumbling down the street and thought it would be cool to hang off the side of it. Later in my childhood, my dreams grew somewhat larger as I announced to my mother that I was going to be a truck driver. I was enchanted with the idea of driving from coast to coast, sleeping at various rest areas along the interstate in the cabin of the big rig and seeing the world through the open canvas of a windshield. At that time in my life, I was more than dreaming. I was asking myself what all human beings eventually ask themselves during their lifetime: What is my purpose?

I was a typical boy who loved sports. I enjoyed playing outside with my friends, riding bikes, going to the pool and watching shows like *Bonanza*. I loved getting my hands dirty, went to church because my parents made me and told my father that, when I grew up, I was going to marry my mom. My childhood was so memorable, in so many positive and reinforcing ways, because of two incredible parents and two younger brothers. I'm sure there were times when I took this love for granted; but, looking back now, I realize how blessed I was to have such an amazing family.

In 1976, my father announced to the family that we were moving to Black Mountain, a town 20 minutes east of Asheville, North Carolina. Although I was initially devastated upon hearing the news, the move proved to be one of the most pivotal moments in my life, as well as for my family. I will always consider Black Mountain to be my hometown. The friendships I made and many of the experiences from my formative years have already been laid out in my first book. However, the greatest gift that Black Mountain gave to me personally was the Black Mountain Golf Course and the introduction of golf into my life.

To say that I was addicted to golf would be an understatement. For the first time in my life, I not only had a dream, but a singular focus — to become a PGA TOUR player. My dream was to win the Masters. "What a story that would make," I thought to myself, "a kid born in Augusta, Georgia, who grows up to be the Masters champion!" In my mind's eye, I could see myself playing Augusta National, making the long walk up the steep inclined fairway of the hole named "Holly," through the towering Georgia pines and up to the 18th green. I could hear the loud ovation from the patrons after my second shot landed safely on the two-tiered green. All I would need was a two-putt to secure the victory, and the green jacket would be mine. I even thought about who I would thank and what I would say during the interview in Butler Cabin. I still recall that dream from time to time, especially during early April, as the world of golf's attention focuses on the Masters.

During my teenage years, my dreams grew even larger. I remember watching my second favorite tournament, the United States Open, with wide eyes and anticipation. The U.S. Open that sticks out the most to me was in 1980. I vividly remember watching Jack Nicklaus make the final birdie putt to beat Isao Aoki on the 18th hole by two shots at Baltusrol Golf Club in Springfield, New Jersey. "Jack is back" was later posted on the scoreboard as Nicklaus raised his major title bar one notch higher.

Looking back at 1980, I can now plainly see how my childhood dreams, God's will and the realities of real life were like stars coming into perfect alignment. The first star that aligned in 1980 was a person, my childhood hero Jack Nicklaus. Jack's career was a major influence on my love for the game. In 1980 at the age of 40, Jack not only won the U.S. Open, but later that summer won the Professional Golfers Association (PGA) Championship on the East Course at Oak Hill Country Club, in Rochester, New York. The fact that my childhood hero won two majors in one year poured gasoline on the fire of my dreams and became a catalyst for shaping my teenage life. Thirty-three years later in 2013, I walked those same hallowed grounds of the East Course at Oak Hill Country Club during the 95th PGA Championship, not as a participant, but as a swing coach for Bob Sowards. It was my third of four appearances with Bob as his swing coach at the PGA Championship and a week I will never forget. As I walked the course with Bob that week, my mind sometimes drifted back to 1980 and Jack Nicklaus. I thought about the shots he played that year while winning the PGA Championship and the fact that I was walking inside the ropes, on the exact same fairways and greens where my dream was born.

The year 1980 proved significant in my life in another way, as Jack Nicklaus and my future mentor, Phil Rodgers, were united as player and coach. Phil was a major influence in both my teaching and personal life. I met Phil in 1992, 12 years after Nicklaus' historic two-major season in 1980, at the Grand Cypress Academy of Golf in Orlando, Florida. I worked under Phil and our director of instruction, Fred Griffin, for 20 years as an instructor at Grand

Cypress. In 1980, Nicklaus called his longtime friend and five-time PGA TOUR winner, Phil Rodgers, to ask for some much-needed short game help. Jack asked Phil to come to his house for two days; Phil stayed for two weeks. Every day, the two men would work on Jack's short game and fish. I would often ask Phil questions like, "What did you work on with Jack's short game?" or "Where did he need the most help?" Phil, however, was more interested in talking about how many fish they caught and less interested in answering my questions. My best guess after hearing Phil recount the story, with a boyish smile written across his face, was that there was more fishing and less practice toward the end of the two weeks. By the year's end, Jack gave credit to Phil for reviving his career with his short game help, after Nicklaus had planted his lips on not one but two major championship trophies that year.

As a man who now looks back through the rearview mirror at my childhood dreams with 20/20 hindsight, my career journey seems crystal clear. My trade over most of my adult life has been teaching golf. I became a PGA member in 1997 and love helping struggling golfers weed through the engrained bad habits that have plagued them for years. I also enjoy working with aspiring young players, whose dreams are to reach higher levels and who are blessed with the talent to take them there. Over my career, I have worked with players of all levels and realize that no two students are alike, just like no two swings are alike. I now get more excited about my student's game than my own, and care less about the scores I shoot. The transition of letting go of my own dreams to foster the dreams of others has not been easy and took time over many years, but I am now at peace with how life has played out. Like the pruning of a tree, getting rid of the old allowed new life and opportunity to blossom. Dreams for our lives can be like a carrot that God uses to lead His children down unimaginable pathways, whether it be during a career change, starting new relationships or with our walk in faith.

God speaks to each of His children differently, at different stages in life and in different ways. Each faith journey is unique and, for me personally, God was speaking loud and clear. His voice was not speaking to me during a church service or while meditating in an open field under a tree, but while I was standing in front of a student teaching the game I love. New, exciting and unexpected miracles started taking place in my mind when God began revealing His dreams for my life. I started noticing that every time I taught a lesson, stories from my life came flooding into my mind. This experience had never happened to me before. I was praying for God to meet my monetary needs, to repair a struggling marriage and lead my career, but instead of answering my prayers the way I expected, He simply answered with more stories. I knew the stories from my life were coming to me from God, but I had no idea why. "What am I going to do with this story?" I thought to myself. "These stories will not pay the bills or save my marriage," as the left side of my brain rationalized with the right.

The stories kept coming for years and would not go away, until I finally acknowledged the obvious: God wanted me to write a book. At first, I resisted with a resounding "No!" I tried my best to ignore what God was giving me and explained to Him that I did not have the education, the talent, the desire nor the dream to take on such a monumental task. This mental exchange with God went on for years until my life hit rock bottom. My divorce now final, God had me exactly where He wanted me. He had my full attention as I made the decision to turn my life back over to Christ. I was sitting at the bottom of a very deep barrel as I looked up with tears in my eyes and prayed, "Father, I will write this book, but you have to lead the way." In 2012, I began the writing journey for my first book and rededicated my life to the Lord. I submitted and for the first time relinquished the leadership role for my life while becoming a follower of Jesus Christ.

This change in my life led to more time studying the Word of God, the Bible. Recently, I read Matthew 10. In this chapter, Jesus gathered His 12 disciples and, for the first time, gave them ***"authority over unclean spirits, to cast them out, and to heal every disease and infirmity" (Matthew 10:1).*** Jesus' instruction to His disciples was to heal only the "lost sheep of Israel" and not the gentiles; that would come later. They were to go from town to town, with no plan or itinerary, and receive no gold or silver for their services. "Where will we sleep and eat?" "Who am I to heal the sick?" "Why would anyone listen to me?" I am sure these are some of the questions that were running through the disciples' minds. While reading Matthew 10, I was able to relate to how the disciples must have felt. The word that came to my mind immediately was "unqualified." When God flooded my mind with stories, I felt unqualified. When I knew in my heart, He wanted me to write a Christian book, I felt unqualified. When I started my book tour, I felt unqualified and when I sat in churches with men and women, young and old, and led the Bible study, I felt unqualified.

In Matthew 10, the disciples were given vague instructions from Jesus for a reason. Jesus was testing the disciples by putting them into situations where they felt unqualified. Jesus was teaching them what faith is all about. None of the original 12 disciples were physicians, and none of them had ever performed miracles; they had only witnessed miracles performed by the Son of God. I can only imagine how insecure they must have felt when Jesus commissioned them to go and cast out demonic forces and heal the sick. Jesus was preparing His disciples for the long and difficult journey ahead by teaching them to trust and to have faith in Him. The boldness to answer the difficult questions or the healing miracles needed to heal the sick and the lame would come from the Spirit of God Almighty, through the disciples to those in need.

In some smaller way, Matthew 10 reminds me of how I felt when God asked me to become an author. Once I yielded to His desire and started writing, my mind opened and the stories flowed out onto the computer screen. I learned that if God asks you to do it and you respond, it will be done. There is no force in the universe powerful enough to stop God's plan for your life except one. That force is free will, given to us by our Creator, to say "no" to His plan for your life. I resisted and said "no" for many years, but found that God is patient. I am so thankful for His patience with my hardheadedness and am so thankful I reconsidered.

I realize that my dreams from 1980 did not come to fruition. I never walked the steep incline of the 18th hole at Augusta National or tapped in the winning putt at the Masters. I have never worn the green jacket or stood before the world as Masters champion. Although I was disappointed when I realized that professional golf as a participant was not where God was leading me, I am thankful my dreams were not part of His plan. Had I won the Masters, I would have thanked my family, my friends and my swing coach, but I would not have thanked God. During my interview in Butler Cabin, I would have told the world about my dreams and hard work, but not given the glory to the One who created me, who instilled those dreams into my DNA and the One who died for my sins, my Savior Jesus Christ.

The writing process has taught me the difference between following the dreams from 1980 and listening to what God was asking me to do. God used my dreams from 1980 to lead me to the game of golf. This experience inspired me into a career as a PGA teaching professional and allowed me to experience some highs along with many lows with the game as both a player and teacher. My dream has led me into an amazing career and brought wonderful people and exciting experiences into my life through the game. Ultimately, this career path allowed me to make a great living, doing what I enjoy doing, while helping struggling golfers along the way.

However, I know that as satisfying as my career has been as a PGA member, there was — and sometimes still is — an empty void in my heart. By following my dreams, I was for the most part taking from the world by trading my time for money. This trading of time for money, over time, leads to a void inside the heart that can only be filled by God. When I let go of my own dreams, submitted to God's plan and became an author, I was no longer trading time for money; I was now spending my time with the Lord. Ben Hogan, a man known to spend countless hours a day practicing alone on a driving range, once said, "There is not enough daylight in any one day to practice everything you need in golf." By writing my first book, I realized the same could be said about our time with the Holy Spirit.

For the first time in my life, I felt as though I had found my niche, my purpose, and knew that my life had changed forever. I realized that the dreams from 1980 were important in my life because they inspired me, but ultimately those dreams were not what would define my life. I now understand that my purpose is ultimately defined by God's plan and my obedience to follow it. My former dreams, combined with my life experiences, teaching knowledge and the words God gave me through the Holy Spirit, became the recipe for my writing. I learned that no matter your trade or the skillset you obtain in this lifetime, we are all called to use what God has given us to glorify Him. Do I still feel unqualified? The answer is "yes." Just as the disciples went out to heal the sick and cast out demons in the name of Jesus Christ, I now sit in front of a computer and ask the Holy Spirit to lead me. This book is a reflection of where He has led me to this point in time.

CHAPTER 2

PURPOSE

"Jesus said, 'Take away the stone.'" (John 11:39)

As a young boy, full of boundless energy and naivety, I would arrive at the Black Mountain Golf Course in anticipation of a full day of golf. Our public course had no driving range, so for me, I would take a few practice swings with my Toney Penna persimmon driver, hit a few putts on the putting green and gather with my friends to tee it up for our daily 36-hole marathon. Later in life, I became a PGA teaching professional at the Grand Cypress Academy of Golf. This move south to Orlando after college allowed me to experience some of the finer things in life.

I had graduated from a public course playground to a golfing haven, a tropical oasis for the golfing enthusiast, with a dual driving range, practice holes and all the latest video technology available at the time. Every day, I would watch my childhood heroes, tour players like Payne Stewart and hundreds of others of the world's greatest players, honing their short games and grooving their almost flawless swings. I was in heaven!

I have been on both sides of the tracks, the public course of my youth and the golfing haven I worked at for two decades. As a PGA professional, I have observed hundreds of thousands of golf swings and taught countless lessons. I have learned the difficult lessons the game has to offer and been privileged to have worked under mentors during my career who showed me the correct path when I lost my way. My journey has taught me many lessons and led me to Columbus, Ohio, where I now am the director of instruction at the Medallion Club. When I now walk onto the driving range, I ask myself one simple question: "What is my purpose for being there?"

In my opinion, there are three reasons why you go to the driving range. The first is to warm up. A tour player's main objective when hitting balls before the round is to loosen up. It is critical that a player use this time to feel the rhythm of the swing, get a feel for the wind and weather, as well as see the ball flight. The second reason is to take a lesson. The driving range is where most of my lessons are given. The lesson time on the range is where the swing can be built from scratch or repaired for the struggling golfer. It is a time when thinking of the swing and its movements are allowed. The third reason is to practice. Practice can occur after a round, days before a tournament or after work.

These three defined purposes for going to the driving range are beneficial when used correctly, but when used incorrectly, they can destroy a player's golf swing. For example, warming up prior to your round is not the time to gather a quick tip from a pro or try to implement what you learned from an instructional video. If the lesson is not ingrained, it will not work on the course. Taking a lesson prior to playing golf is usually a recipe for disaster. Have a plan when you get to the practice range and then put in the needed work. Practicing is encouraged, but resist the temptation to beat balls for an hour; instead, take time to cover all aspects of your game. By defining the purpose and working on the purpose of why you are there, your time will be maximized and the results will be better.

In the game of life, I have struggled like everyone in finding or defining my purpose. God's plan for my life was not to be a PGA TOUR player but rather a teacher of the game, a role that I love. But there are days when I ask myself, "Is this all there is to my life? Is my purpose only to teach golf?" When I see the word "purpose," I think of the word "work." When it comes to one's life purpose, I now think of two words: "God's purpose."

One day while reading the David Jeremiah Study Bible, I learned a valuable lesson from Dr. Jeremiah about purpose and work. I read one of my favorite stories about the resurrection of

Lazarus. In the Gospel of John, Jesus' friend Lazarus had been dead for days and placed in a tomb. Before the miracle occurred, Jesus asked the people to move the stone that covered the tomb. In this famous story, the stone represents the work that needed to be done by the people before the miracle would occur. In other words, God has a purpose for each one of us. The people could have said, "I'm not moving that heavy stone! The man has been dead for days!" Had that response occurred, who knows if the miracle would have taken place? But instead of laziness or reluctance, the people instead had faith and, without hesitation, the miracle was birthed from apparent death.

I now know that one of my stones to be moved in my life was the writing of my first book. I knew God was asking me to write it, but I was scared because I was not an author and the task seemed insurmountable! The key was trusting what God was asking me to do and then taking the most difficult first step, the removal of the stone. God's purpose for our lives often requires that we become a verb and are put into action. Once I started, the Holy Spirit took over, and the floodgates of my mind opened, ran through my fingertips and gave birth to countless stories onto the computer screen. The stone now removed, God's miracle came to print four years later.

Before you arrive at the driving range, define the purpose of why you are there, move the stone and get to work. Then trust the process. In the game of life, ask God to define your purpose, wait for Him to guide your step, then move the stone! Your success and miracle may or may not be measured by the world where we currently live, but doing work that glorifies God from the fairways of earth always leads to amazing scores on the leaderboard in Heaven.

Golf Tips Magazine Sept/Oct 2021 Issue

CHAPTER 3

THE REFLECTION

"And we all, with unveiled face, beholding the glory of the Lord, are being transformed into the same image from one degree of glory to another. For this comes from the Lord who is the Spirit." (2 Corinthians 3:18)

As a teenage boy, I could not wait for the various golf magazines to come to the house. I would grab the magazine from the mailbox and immediately gravitate to the many swing sequences of the game's greatest players, read the advice from golf's most prominent teachers, and then grab my club and head to the mirror. I would gaze into the looking glass and emulate every position I saw that month, and then it was out to my personal driving range, my front yard. "This tip will make the difference," I thought to myself — that is, until next month's periodicals arrived. The magazine was my new swing tip, the mirror my Top 100 teacher and the reflection my answer. Looking back at my life, I believe this time of seeking the so-called "perfect swing" in front of the full-length mirror was more than teenage vanity; it was a moment in life that gave birth to my first real passion, the game of golf.

Golf is the ultimate reflection of hard work, dedication, technique, courage, talent, technology, psychology, creativity and touch, plus a lifetime of practice. It is impossible to name all the skills needed to play this great game. One of the things I love most about golf is the game's unique ability to make visible a player's strengths and weaknesses, and there is no better example of this than the scorecard. Simply put, in golf the player is ultimately judged by the score.

During the early years of my golfing career, I was certainly putting in the time and hard work needed to improve, but on the course, the scores said otherwise. For some reason, I was not maximizing my time, and my results showed it. It was not until I met the late Jesse Haddock, the legendary three-time NCAA championship head coach at Wake Forest University, that I started learning the importance of keeping statistics after the round. Coach Haddock stressed the importance of looking at the numbers within the number on the scorecard, and like any good accountant will tell you, "The numbers never lie." This time spent counting my greens in regulation, fairways hit and number of putts, just to name a few, is when I realized why my scores were higher than desired. The scorecard was my mirror, the stats were my top 100 teacher as well as my guide to where my practice time would be spent.

When I think of my passions now, perfecting my golf swing and lowering my scores has fallen way down the priority list. It has been replaced by the passion to teach the game, as well as a newfound, unexpected and creative passion of writing. But these passions pale in comparison to the most important passion in my life today, loving the Lord. During a recent time of meditation, God spoke to my heart, revealing His wisdom, the wisdom I had been praying to receive over the last several years. I immediately grabbed a pen and paper and began writing His words.

"If you want to know what God looks like, give food to the poor, provide them shelter and love your neighbor. Embrace those you disagree with and say 'thank you' to a stranger. If you want to see His reflection, help someone in need. We are all bits and pieces of God. God loves the prostitute who works to feed her addiction, just as much as the man who puts a 50 in the offering plate."

When I look at my swing now on high-speed video and gather launch monitor data, I can still see some of the same flaws of that teenage boy standing in front of the mirror with his golf magazine. When I get the opportunity to play a quick nine holes, I still look over my scorecard with a fine-tooth comb, reflecting on each hole played as a teacher first and participant second. The reflection of today's technology and the scorecard can be difficult to stomach at times, reminding me that no swing or round of golf is perfect. But, when I see my fellow man giving to others, I see God. Although man can never be perfect in front of the mirror of life, for a moment in time, the world is shown a reflection that is awfully close. When we give to others in need, we are transformed and show the reflection of our Lord and Savior Jesus Christ. Want to look good in front of the mirror? Help your fellow man during their time of need, shine your light and let others see the reflection of God!

Golf Tips Magazine May/June 2021 Issue

Chapter 4

The Perfect Shot

"For all have sinned and fall short of the glory of God."
(Romans 3:23)

The first time I saw my golf swing on video, I was a skinny teenager, full of insecurities that were camouflaged by a thick layer of persistence. I was enjoying my first true experience of golf supervision at the Wake Forest Golf Camp in Winston-Salem, North Carolina. Our housing for the week was the Arnold Palmer/Brian Piccolo Dormitory. During our first day of camp, our instructor filmed our group's swing one by one, and later that night we all met back in the dormitory to review the first-day results. One by one, our counselor showed the picturesque swings of the other students, praising the technique of players who were older in age and more experienced with their form. It was obvious that this was not the first time they had received instruction or seen their swings on video. I had never seen my swing on video and was excited to see what the camera revealed. I impatiently waited, wondering, "What will I look like?" "Will my swing measure up to the others?" Unlike today where selfies and video cameras are shot in an instant with a cell phone, video at the time was a fairly new technology used in teaching. Our swings that day were not seen on the flat screen of a computer but were analyzed with a VHS tape on a black-and-white television.

Finally, it was my time to be critiqued under the watchful eye of my instructor. As soon as he hit play, I was in shock! Like the fizz of a Coca-Cola rising to the top of a cold glass, my insecurities came pouring out. I was in total disbelief of how skinny, unorthodox and unathletic my technique looked compared to the other more athletic swings. In my mind, the other swings were poetry in motion compared to mine. I began to feel tears well up in my eyes and even heard a few snickers, or so I thought. Like a raging river, the list of swing changes, too many to remember, came flowing out of my instructor's mouth. Later that night, I went back to my dorm room and cried myself to sleep. The next morning, I awoke full of determination, with a new chip resting directly on my right shoulder, with one goal in mind. I was now in quest of the perfect golf swing.

Fast forward to the early 1990s when I moved to Orlando, Florida, and started working at the Grand Cypress Academy of Golf. I began my entry-level work picking the driving range. I will never forget my orientation day when I first saw the seasoned teaching professionals teaching the game that I loved. At that moment, I was struck with a bolt of lightning, a passion and a knowing that teaching golf was what I was destined to do with my life. I fell head over heels in love with teaching and, for the first time in my 25 years of life, knew that I wanted to be a PGA golf instructor.

Working for minimum wage at a world-renowned golf school did have its advantages. Free golf, the best practice facilities in the world, tour players walking through the doors daily and teaching technology like I had never seen. I knew I wanted to be a great teacher, like those I was working under during my apprenticeship, but for me to get approval from my peers, my golf swing had to improve. Luckily for me, God had put me in the right place to make me better, both as a teacher and a player. I was now in the perfect place, a golfing oasis, ready to take my pursuit of the perfect swing to the next level.

Over time, my swing improved dramatically, and the video showed it. I became obsessed with how my swing looked on camera and hitting perfect shots. Looking back, I never let go of those "snickers" in my mind from golf camp and used that moment as motivation to reach higher levels. I began competing in mini tour events and attempted qualifying for larger tournaments. In my book, *Golf Is My Life: Glorifying God Through the Game*, I describe one of my many attempts to try to qualify for the U.S. Open. I was standing in the middle of the fairway on my 18th hole. My approach shot was to a tucked pin with water in front of the green, to the left and over the green. I was even-par for the day, needing birdie to advance to the next stage. My ball was 123 yards from the pin, into the wind, so I chose a 9 iron. In the book, I wrote the following excerpt:

"The wind was howling, and the flag rippled so much that I could hear it from the fairway. I honestly wasn't nervous; I had worked my entire life to hit this shot and the conditions were ripe for me to be aggressive and let it go. I took one last look at my target 20 feet right of the hole and made my swing. As I hit the ball, I had a sincere feeling of ecstasy, because it was perfect. As the ball bore through the air, it started to move from right to left from my natural shot shape and the slope of the fairway. I said to my caddie Chevis, 'That's perfect!'

At that moment, in my mind, my hard work had paid off. I had reached my goal and I was going to take the next step forward as a player. I had hit the perfect shot. But instead, I was about to learn a difficult life lesson. Let's continue with the story:

"The wind caught the draw and straightened the ball's flight. It hovered straight at the flagstick. I was so excited watching the shot that for an instance eagle popped into my head. The ball came down and I wondered if it might fly in the hole. Suddenly, I heard a loud clank and the ball disappeared for a second. The small gallery behind the green yelled, 'It hit the flag!'

I looked up in amazement as the ball hit the top of the flagstick and flew vertically back into the air 20 feet above the flagstick. My heart came out of my chest because it appeared from my angle to fly straight up into the air. I thought to myself, 'That's all right. It will roll back down the hill toward the hole.' Unfortunately, the ball flew too far over the green and rested on a patch of St. Augustine grass, six inches from the water. I threw down my hat in disgust and let out several profanities."

I went on to make double bogey that day and missed advancing by several shots. I had some long nights that week and once again cried myself to sleep, this time as a grown man. My pursuit of the perfect swing and the perfect shot, or so I thought, had now turned into a life lesson. Now, with a touch of silver and recession in my hairline, I look back on that moment, not with anger but gratitude. The difficult lessons that I experienced in my pursuit of perfection have taught me one important lesson. Perfection does not exist in golf or in this lifetime.

No swing is perfect, and although we may at times hit perfect shots, the game of golf is simply a "what have you done for me lately kind of game." You may be currently standing in the middle of the fairway, but you still must execute the next shot. My obsession to be perfect has now changed to acceptance, the acceptance that my life and my golf swing will never be perfect and the acceptance that sometimes life isn't fair. This acceptance for my life is not punishment for a job not well done but maturity and growth.

I will never be perfect as a man, I will never be a perfect teacher and I will never have a perfect golf swing or play a perfect round of golf. Looking back at my pursuit of the perfect swing, I now realize there are only four things that are perfect. First is God Almighty, the Father, maker of Heaven and Earth. Second is the perfect person, Jesus Christ, a man who not only lived without sin but a Savior who died for my sins. Third is the Holy Spirit, God Almighty, living inside of my heart and soul and guiding me. Finally, there is a destination of perfection called Heaven, a believer's final home and a place that I long for in my heart and mind.

As I now play the fairways of my life, I sometimes find the center. But on the days when I am not in the short grass, surrounded by trees, water or sand, I think of my Savior and Heaven. My fairways of life will one day lead to the perfect place, Heaven, as well as to God and His Son Jesus Christ. By putting my faith in my Savior, I no longer measure life by my futile attempts at perfect work. As it states in the scriptures, through repentance, my faith in Jesus makes up for where I have fallen short.

In many ways, Jesus and the lessons learned from the game of golf are very similar. The beauty of the golf course, played with family and friends on a sunny day, gives us the opportunity to have a slice of Heaven. Although our swings may not be perfect and our ball is sometimes lost, we have an opportunity waiting in the form of the next shot. Once we safely find the green, the struggles sometimes continue, bringing grown men to the brink of tears while others rejoice with praise as their golf ball disappears into the cup. In the scorecard of life, repentance for our shortcomings to our Savior is like a great day with the flat stick after a few errant shots. I guess the ol' saying really is true: "Putting does make up for a lot of sins."

Golf Tips Magazine Jan/Feb 2022 Issue

CHAPTER 5

THE INNER VOICE

"I can do all things through Christ who strengthens me."
(Philippians 4:13)

In the spring of 1983, I made my first appearance in the state tournament at Finley Golf Course in Chapel Hill, North Carolina. To say I was a bit nervous would be an understatement, considering the prior year I was the sixth man on our team, with limited playing experience. On top of that, it was the first time in school history our high school had qualified for the state tournament. I've always said to my students who play tournament golf, "The nerves you feel on the first tee are the same nerves the tour players feel. The difference is the tour players are used to it." As I stood on the first tee, I could feel my knees shaking and a lump the size of a golf ball forming in my throat. When the starter announced, "Next on the tee from Charles D. Owen High School… Jon Decker," I could literally hear my heart beating through my sweat-stained shirt.

I teed the ball up on the left side of the tee box in anticipation of my natural right-to-left ball flight. I went through my pre-shot routine, looked at my target and made an aggressive swing. Solid contact and my ball went flying down the middle. "Whew!" I thought to myself as I gasped for air. Normally after the first shot, I begin to relax, but today was different. I stood over my approach shot, made my swing and immediately knew I was in trouble. I dead-cold shanked the ball into the right rough. Luckily, no spectators were hit as I bowed my head in shame. Fast-forward to the second hole, another shank, and several holes later yet another. Suddenly, without invite, I had a new playing companion that joined my threesome, one who would conveniently speak up as I set up to hit each shot. My new competitor was a voice in my head, a voice that only I could hear. "Don't shank it," whispered the voice as I attempted to initiate the backswing. That late spring day in Chapel Hill, I lost all semblance of my golf swing and was rudely introduced to a one-sided conversation in my mind. I soon began to realize that day that this voice was certainly not my friend.

I have learned in life one very simple principle. If you have thoughts that are negative or counterproductive, they are not from God. If you worry, it's not from God. If you have a voice that says, "You're not good enough, you're ugly or you'll never find someone," it's not from God. I believe there is only one God and I also believe there is an enemy, an evil force that so often is referred to in the Bible as "the deceiver." Golf is like life, the ultimate game played in the mind first, then executed on the golf course second. Learning to quiet the mind and allow the body to perform takes years to perfect and is never mastered. I have spent my entire life trying to master this concept of mind and body, two forces working in tandem to execute one single shot at a time.

As a child, I would watch every tournament on television, especially the majors. There are some that I remember more than others, like Nicklaus winning the Masters in 1986 and Tiger winning the U.S. Open in 2000. But for me, there is one tournament that stands out. Not for the player or the event, but because of what his interview taught me after he won. In 2015, I was watching the British Open at Carnoustie and a four-hole playoff between Zach Johnson, Louis Oosthuizen and Marc Leishman. Johnson survived the playoff to win his second major tournament. During an emotional interview with tears streaming down his face, Johnson said, "I kept saying scripture all day long." Zach's statement affected me profoundly. I immediately realized that when I played competitive golf, I was not saying scripture; I was in a mental argument with my inner voice. Zach Johnson relied on his golf swing to physically win the British Open that day, but in my opinion, the reason he won was not because of the physical swing. It was because he made the choice to say scripture to himself, during one of the most pressure-packed weeks of his life. Zach chose to use the Word of God to block out the negative chatter that he knew could creep into his mind and affect his golf swing.

I recently read a book by my friend Alecia Larson, a teaching professional from Pensacola, Florida. In her book, *The Missing Link: The Powerful Role of Self-Talk in the Mind Game of Golf*, Alecia talks about the inner voice. In the book she states, *"If your inner voice were a person, would you be friends with him or her?"* When I read that statement, I had a breakthrough because it reminded me of the 1983 state tournament and my "new friend" saying to me as I was trying to hit my approach shot, "Don't shank it."

In early spring of 2013, I began my writing journey for my first book. I learned that the most difficult part of the writing journey was getting started, but once I did, the words came pouring out. However, at night my old friend, the one I had met back at the state tournament, would join me at my bedside and the one-sided conversations began to flow like a river. "You've never written a book! You're a golf pro, not an author! Even if you wrote the book, who would publish it? Who would read it?" This conversation went on night after night until I said, "Enough!" So, one night as I got into bed, I began verbally speaking, ***"I can do all things through Christ who strengthens me."*** I repeated, ***"I can do all things through Christ who strengthens me."*** I did this repeatedly until my nemesis cowered away. I chose that verse, **Philippians 4:13**, to be the initial scripture in my first book.

I now rely on a new inner voice in my life, one that I welcome with open arms. He is the Holy Spirit. By accepting Jesus as my Lord and Savior, I know that He lives inside of me. The enemy will often use deception in spiritual warfare, so if the voice I hear makes me uncomfortable, I mentally pull out scripture and speak it repeatedly. If the inner voice is productive and guiding me, then I know it is from the Lord. I often use this guidance in my writing for my *Golf Tips Magazine* feature *Fairways to Heaven* or when preparing for public speaking engagements. I ask the Lord to give me the words because words do have power. I know that the Word of God can offset any sudden attack from the enemy. Oh, how I wish I had used this arsenal of weapons from the Bible while competing on the mini tours of Florida so many years ago.

One of the greatest gifts God gives to each of us is free will. We can choose how we think, we can choose our friends, we can choose what words we say to ourselves. Choose to listen to those words and ask yourself, "Are these words from God?" If not, be like Zach Johnson and invite the Word of God to be a part of your daily routine. Use the Word of God to inspire you to help others or to calm your mind when standing over a difficult three-foot putt with everything on the line. Words do have power! I often tell my students that, ultimately, you will become in life what you think about yourself. Choose to speak positive words of affirmation and faith over the negative barrage of words that come to you, whether it is from television, social media or while sitting in rush hour traffic.

In 1983, I was introduced to an unfamiliar force, an inner voice, that was foreign to me at the time. I'm sure the inner voice had been with me in my early childhood, but it took the pressure of the state tournament to fully bring him out. For the first time in my life, I really got to know the enemy, and it wasn't a fair fight! I had no weapons. I cowardly played the first 27 of 36 holes that year, hitting a shank every two or three holes. Then something happened as I stood on the 28th hole, ready to play my last nine. I stopped listening to the voice and made up my mind to just have fun and play golf. I hit every green in regulation and shot an even-par 36. On the four-hour drive home from the tournament, I reflected on the round knowing I could do it. I chose to not give up and to use that experience to become a better player. I often reflect on that experience when teaching golfers of all levels. As humans, we all have an enemy and, if we allow the enemy to sabotage our mind, the battle will be lost for the day.

I am now sobered by the fact that a large part of why I never truly reached my lofty goals as a professional golfer was not because of my physical golf swing but because I listened to those unwelcome voices. The lessons learned since my tournament playing days have taught me how to combat spiritual warfare and win the battle. This battle is won not by my strength but through the Lord's. Looking in the rear-view mirror of life, the words spoken to me by the enemy were nothing but lies. How do I know this fact? I know my book was published every time I open it. I know the book was read when someone reaches out to say how much they enjoyed it. I know I am an author every time I open a *Golf Tips Magazine* and see my article *Fairways to Heaven.* These are the facts of my life, and I am so thankful I learned to use the Word of God to drown out the lies. Give those unwelcome voices to the Lord, live each day to win the battle, then give the glory to God!

Golf Tips Magazine May/June 2022 Issue

Chapter 6

Going Low

"This is the day the Lord has made; We will rejoice and be glad in it." (Psalm 118:24)

I vaguely remember the first time I broke 100 at my home course, the Black Mountain Golf Course. Although I was not yet in high school, that day I was able to manage my homemade swing up and down the mountainous fairways, taking advantage of a few fortunate bounces and seeing the ball find the bottom of the cup more times than not. The excitement I felt as I made my way home on my bicycle was followed by the question my father so often asked after I told him my score, "Jon, did you putt everything out?" Later that summer, I noticed my scores suddenly going lower, and I asked myself, "Can I break 90?" A few years later in high school, the 80s became the norm for my scorecard, and all I could see on the horizon of my mind were the 70s. By my sophomore year, the scores in the 70s were beginning to firmly take root, and the lower I went, the better it felt. Setting my bar lower became my goal, and in golf there is no better feeling than reaching lower levels of unfamiliar ground. But there was one level in golf I had only heard about from the more experienced players, and getting there would take more than a few fortunate bounces. The lessons I learned from the experience have lasted a lifetime and shaped the way I now teach when working with a player's mindset on the golf course. It was time for me to go low, to reach new heights in my game. It was time for me to taste the 60s!

During my late teenage years, if I walked off the golf course and shot over a 75, I was somewhere between heartbroken and furious. I would stew all night in bed after a poor round and host my own ESPN SportsCenter recapping the day's highlights. These mental conversations included catch phrases about my "what ifs" and "should have" shots, and let us not forget about my bad kicks and lip-outs. I had all my excuses on the tip of my tongue as I painstakingly explained every shot from the day to both my parents. Looking back, I'm sure after a long day of work and raising three boys, the last thing my mom and dad wanted to do was to lace up their golf shoes and replay every shot of my round. I had reached even-par 71 on my home track, but I had yet to break par until one summer day. I shot a one-under par 70 and broke par for the very first time, and yet I still wasn't satisfied. I "should have" shot lower!

The next week, I walked off the 17th hole with a birdie and stood on the 18th tee box at 2 under par. I remember telling myself, "All you have to do is par the last hole and you break 70!" After walking off number 18 green with a bogey, I was in disbelief! I couldn't figure out what I had done wrong. The next week I stood on number 18 tee box and began adding up my score. All I needed was a par to break 70, but once again I walked off number 18 with a bogey. I was furious! A few days later, I stood on number 18 tee box and said to myself, "Jon, you have parred this hole a thousand times in your life. Focus on the next shot." I hit my drive straight down the middle. I then focused on my second shot, not my score, and the ball came to rest on the middle of the green. Now it was time to focus on my speed, and I rolled the birdie putt next to the hole. I tapped in for par and walked off the green with a 2-under total of 69. At that moment I realized why I hadn't succeeded in the past. I realized there wasn't a physical reason why I couldn't go lower in the past; it was all mental. I had been living in the future on the golf course and living in the past at home in bed instead of focusing on the task at hand.

After my first book was released, I was asked to speak to the First Tee in Dallas, Texas. During the speech, I shared one of my favorite quotes. I heard the quote originally during a radio interview from the former defensive coordinator for the East Carolina University Pirates football team, Rick Smith. Coach Smith used this quote often after a bad game or when the team gave up a big play: *"Yesterday is history and tomorrow is a mystery, but today is a gift from God. That's why we call it the present. In other words, today is God's gift to you."* I believe that this ability to focus on today, the moment you are in today and the shot you are getting ready to execute next is what separates the elite athletes, no matter what the sport. In the recent documentary about the Chicago Bulls dynasty, *The Last Dance*, the author of the book *Rare Air*, Mark Vancil, states in describing Michael Jordan, *"Most people live in fear because we project the past into the future. Michael's a mystic. He was never anywhere else. His gift was not that he could run fast, jump high or shoot a basketball. His gift was that he was completely present."*

In the game of life, focusing on the present moment can be challenging. Fear and worry of the future or reliving our mistakes from the past are recipes for stress, lack of sleep, depression and, in some severe cases, even suicide. As ***Psalm 118:24 so beautifully states, "This is the day the Lord has made; We will rejoice and be glad in it."*** Every day God spoon-feeds us one breath at a time, as well as the perfect amount of His grace. The challenge we all face during our journey in this lifetime and the challenges we face as we walk the fairways on the course is to stay in the present moment, one shot and one day at a time. Living in harmony and the moment we are in during our daily journey often requires patience and faith in a higher source. The mistakes of our past shots or the fears of tomorrow do nothing to enhance our present state, and those who choose to live out of the moment are robbed of one of God's most precious gifts: time. Once time is wasted, it can never be relived. This is the day! This is the time to stay in the moment! So, rejoice this day, look up to a higher source, stay in the present shot, and no matter where you are on the course, always try to go low.

Golf Tips Magazine Nov/Dec 2021 Issue

Chapter 7

The Clean Slate

"That, in reference to your former manner of life, you lay aside the old self, which is being corrupted in accordance with the lusts of deceit, and that you be renewed in the spirit of your mind, and put on the new self, which in the likeness of God has been created in righteousness and holiness of the truth." (Ephesians 4:22-24)

In December of 1992, I began my career in the golf business at the Grand Cypress Academy of Golf. Excited to finally have a career direction, I got accustomed to my new golfing paradise that included a dual driving range, three practice holes manicured to PGA TOUR standards, a slew of amazing instructors at my disposal to offer advice as well as the most up-to-date technology in the world to review my golf swing. I was in golf heaven!

Although I was picking the driving range and working in the academy shop, my off time was consumed with shadowing other teachers in the hopes of learning new teaching skills, as well as working on my own game. I had only seen my golf swing a few times in the past, and video technology was in its infancy, so the fact that I could see my swing in slow motion or stop it and critique it was a new and exciting adventure.

Every day I would take time after work to film my swing, go inside to analyze it, ask other teachers for their perspective, then walk outside into the searing Florida heat to hit balls. Now in my late 20s, I came to a crossroads in my career as a young teacher and struggling mini tour player. I made a conscious decision to totally rehabilitate my flawed swing from my teenager years and totally rebuild it from scratch. It was a difficult journey that took years, but looking back, taught me so much about golf instruction. This transformative period of my life reinforced my teaching career in unexpected ways by allowing me to understand how my students felt when they were rehabilitating their own golf swing. I knew it was time for a fresh start. My old swing had run its course, and I knew that to accomplish my goals, I would need a clean slate.

Although my golf swing changes were moving at a snail's pace, my teaching career elevated rapidly. Like today's golf market, the game was on fire during the late 90s. The "Tiger effect" was in full bloom, and golf instructors were in high demand. I had started at the bottom but over time was standing in front of eager students who were hanging on my every word of instruction.

Over time I noticed two types of students. The first was the total beginner. They were starting from a clean slate, and as a result, they had no preconceived idea of what they were supposed to do in the golf swing. Their virgin minds for the game were oblivious to any false information on the swing, like the quick tips I often hear on the range between golfing buddies, just prior to a Saturday morning match. Beginners willing to listen were the ideal students, although they would have never known it. They usually came to the golf schools very timid and shy but, like a well-disciplined child, would trustingly follow my instructions step-by-step, without hesitation or reluctance.

The second student was the lifelong player who comes to the golf school as a last resort. They have one foot in the shallow end of not being able to hit the ball in the air and the other foot in the deep end of yesteryear when their drives were longer and their scores were lower. They would come to the golf schools not timidly like the beginner but fearfully because their slate was not clean. These students were struggling, and they feared the changes to come. I was always amazed at these students because they were paying a lot of money to improve, yet they didn't want to change a thing; for these students, change was their greatest fear. In many ways, the lessons learned from teaching at golf schools taught me a lot about human nature, how we learn and how much extra mental weight we all carry in our daily lives.

In the game of life, we all start out just like the beginning student, born with a clean slate. I see the innocence of children every time I drive by a school playground, seeing them play without a care in the world. I see it when I teach a young junior golfer, some under the age of 4, through their wide eyes as the ball soars through the air. However, like the student who has played and struggled for years, I see those same children's smiles turn to tears of disappointment as their clean slate becomes stained. No longer satisfied with the ball simply getting airborne, frustration begins to set in, followed by tears as their golf ball suddenly curves offline.

Time has a way of chipping away at our childhood innocence in the game of golf as well as the game of life. It starts in the lesson when the beginner student proclaims, "I just want to hit the ball and not embarrass myself," and then they hit the shot of their new golfing lives and they respond, "Now if I could just do that every time!" Human nature has a way of wanting more in life, whether it is longer drives, lower scores, more money in the bank or a larger house, our slate never seems to get cleaner; we just raise the bar, ask for more and then dirty the slate once again.

Although my dreams to play on the tour never came to fruition, I am still teaching the game I love. However, I now have new interests in my life. In 2016, after publishing my first book, I became a senior editor for *Golf Tips Magazine* as well as a public speaker. Writing became a passion in my life and new pathways were formed. My career path was suddenly transformed, unforeseen by a naïve 25-year-old starting out in the golf business. Through prayer, meditation and a lot of self-reflection, I started to mature as a man and felt God's hand slowly start to transform me into the man He intended for me to be.

After the book release came an audiobook. One day, a new author, one with a clean writing slate, reached out to me asking for advice about getting her book published. She asked many wonderful questions, and I did my best to help her; but truthfully, I still consider myself to be a novice, not one to be giving advice. Toward the end of our conversation, she stated, "I want the book to be successful, and I want the book to be profitable." Now I knew the book she was writing is a Christian book, so I responded instinctively, "Jesus walked the earth for 33 years and ministered the last three years of his life, and He never made a penny from it. I too had the same dreams as you for my book to be sold all around the world, making lots of money and using the money to help others." I reminded my friend of the same advice given to me by my first editor, Pete McDaniel, when I dreamt of my book becoming a *New York Times* best seller. Pete said, "Jon, God will put your book into the hands of those He wants to read it."

I believe God has a purpose for every soul on this earth. Our soul is encased in a body that the scriptures refer to as the flesh. Through sin, we all stain the slate that God intended to be so pure. Through repentance of our transgressions to our Savior, Jesus Christ, we are transformed, and the sins He died for are forgiven and our slate is clean. When I chose to rebuild my golf swing, in essence I was starting from a clean slate. I compared each swing to a model and, over time, transformed my swing. I was willing to start over, let go of the old and resist the temptation to go back to my old swing on the course when faced with a difficult shot. Over time, I learned to trust the process, and by the time I was in my mid-30s, my swing and game were transformed.

As a Christian, I have made a choice to put my faith in Jesus Christ. I still have the temptations of this world, but I now have a Savior. The 33-year-old human life of Jesus Christ is now the model for my life. As stated in the scriptures, transformation is part of the Christian's daily walk. I often pray the following: "Father, please transform me into the man You created me to be, in Jesus' name. Amen." I pray these words to remind myself that my efforts are not enough, whether in my quest to perfect my swing, say the exact words needed to a friend seeking advice or write another article or book. I say these words to remind myself that if I give my life to the Lord, I can let go of my old self. As I submit each day, I slowly transform and become one step closer to being more like Jesus and a little less like the man I once thought I should be.

Golf Tips Magazine July/August 2022 Issue

CHAPTER 8

THE BURIED LIE

"*Now godliness with contentment is great gain. For we brought nothing into this world, and it is certain, we can carry nothing out.*" (1 Timothy 6:6-7)

Some of my fondest memories as a PGA teaching professional are from a 20-year span of my life teaching at the Grand Cypress Academy of Golf. Many of these wonderful memories involve teaching with my mentor, Phil Rodgers. Working with Phil was exhilarating, to say the very least, and for the students and the instructors involved, it was more than golf instruction. Teaching with Phil Rodgers was like stepping into a time machine at the World Golf Hall of Fame. It was more than world-class golf instruction; it was a total golf learning experience, at the highest possible level. After all, not many instructors can say that they were invited to the home of Jack Nicklaus to help him revamp his short game from his waterfront estate in North Palm Beach, Florida.

Although I enjoyed asking Phil many questions about his time with Jack, my personal favorite story was when Phil played in the Masters and was paired with Gary Player. I do not recall the year, but both players went for the green in two on the par-5 15th hole named Fire Thorn. Phil and Gary both hit their second shot into the bunker on the right, a bunker that had now collected the balls of two of the greatest bunker players the game has ever known. Gary's ball was on the upslope, a fairly routine shot under normal circumstances, but with a downhill sloped green and pond looming in the background, this shot was anything but routine. Phil's lie, however, was not so fortunate. Only a few feet from

Gary's ball, Phil's ball was buried in the face of the bunker on the downslope — an impossible shot!

I can still hear Phil telling the story: "I knew that if I tried to play toward the green, I would get out, but the ball would roll into the water. If I played backward, it was an easy out, but I couldn't because of the grandstands. So, I said to myself, let's blast the ball hard enough to escape the buried lie and leave it on the upslope of the bunker. I hit the shot perfectly from the buried lie, only advancing it a few feet. The patrons groaned in disbelief, as if the shot had been mishit. I now was in perfect position to play my fourth shot. I blasted the ball and landed it on the front of the green, allowing gravity to roll the ball down the hill. I watched as the ball gathered speed and rolled directly in the hole for a 4. The patrons responded with a smattering of applause, as if the escape had been a lucky break. Gary then got up to play his third shot. Unlike my use of the slope and gravity, Gary flew the ball all the way to the hole, stopping it on a dime with back spin, several feet from the hole. The patrons stood and cheered in approval of his shot execution!" Phil would then always laugh and say, "Gary always got the larger applause, but we both walked off the green with the same score — birdie!"

Years later, I was trying to qualify for the U.S. Open. I was 1 under par playing my 9th hole. My approach shot buried on the downslope of the bunker, and the green was running straight downhill away from me with a pond as my backdrop. Immediately, I thought of Phil Rodgers and what he would say to me if he were there: "Jon, be content to take what the shot gives you. Don't force it and run up your score." Like my mentor, I purposely hit my next shot hard enough to dislodge it from the grip of the sand, advancing it forward to the upslope. I then blasted the ball about 3 feet from the hole and tapped in for a crucial bogey. I went on to shoot 72 that day, missing a playoff by one shot. Although my dream of playing in a U.S. Open did not come to fruition, I learned a valuable lesson that day, one that I will carry with me the rest of my life. In golf and in the game of life, contentment in your present situation, whether good or bad, is the key to success.

Golf teaches you to accept one simple fact — the game is not always fair. Before meeting Phil Rodgers, I would have tried to hit the hero shot, gone in the pond and made a big number. Fortunately for me that day, wisdom prevailed, and as a result, I avoided a disaster. Successful living requires this same discipline. In *1 Timothy,* Paul writes of contentment and later states that *"money is the root of all evil."* How often in life I have looked at my life as if it were a golf ball, buried under the lip of a bunker on a downslope, with a pond of disparity in the background. Oh, how I yearned to be free from those situations. Whether it was my divorce, financial problems or pandemic, my body felt the weight of the chains that appeared to be holding me down.

I now realize the difficult "lies" we all experience in life are part of God's plan. Human instinct is to force our way out, but God asks us to be content in our situation and let Him do the heavy lifting. We live in a world where it is easy to compare our lives to others. Why is my ball buried in the sand and yet my competitor's ball, only a few feet away, has found a perfect lie? Our society craves the lives of the famous, those who seem to have it all, as if the answer to our lives lies in their possessions or the vacations they always seem to take.

In the game of golf, contentment is when you walk off the green knowing you made the best score possible given the situation of each shot. But, just like the game of life, sometimes our walk to the next tee box falls way short of maximizing our opportunities. The game of golf is so similar to the game of life; in golf we get to play another shot and get to play another hole, and in life we get to wake up, start over and live another day. God asks us to be content in every moment, trust Him and live with joy and peace, no matter what our situation.

One day we will all play our final hole, and in that moment as we walk off the green of our lives from a world that is often so unfair, we will be met with an everlasting love. Until then, be content with your present lie, trusting God to deliver you safely on the green, allowing His grace to deliver you to the hole, and walk off the green knowing that you made the best score possible for that day.

Golf Tips Magazine Nov/Dec 2020 Issue

CHAPTER 9

THE FAITHFUL SERVANT

"Take My yoke upon you and learn from Me, for I am gentle and lowly in heart, and you will find rest for your souls. For My yoke is easy and My burden is light." (Mathew 11:29-30)

On a hot summer's day in the late 1990s, I was playing in the North Florida Chapter Championship as a young PGA teaching professional. The event was held at the Timacuan Golf Course in Lake Mary, Florida. I loved the competition of playing in our section events, and for someone who had just turned professional, I looked at these tournaments like they were "majors." They say in life you can only count on two things — "death and taxes." Well, an addendum to that statement might be the heat and humidity of Florida in July. As I walked onto the tee box of the final hole, I started feeling somewhat faint. I was playing well, but the combination of heat, adrenaline and nerves was starting to take its toll. As I look back on that day now, I realize that mentally I was carrying an extra load from the excessive heat, one that led to confusion and uncertainty.

Although I was somewhat out of sorts standing over the ball, I was able to find the middle of the fairway with my tee shot, just past the 150-yard marker. I paced off 3 yards, putting me at 147 yards to the center of the green. I then looked at the pin sheet and started doing the math. I immediately started getting confused; the pin was back left, but I could not do the simple math to come up with my yardage. I had no caddie to rely on as I fumbled with the numbers. "How can I hit my next shot if I don't know my number," I thought to myself. It was now my turn to play, as I felt all eyes staring at me as if to say, "Let's go while we're young!" I was lost and confused in the heat of the moment. Reluctantly I started my pre-shot routine, but there was nothing routine about what I was feeling inside. As I stood over the ball, I am embarrassed to admit that I had not committed to my approach shot and still had no confirmation of the yardage. As one might expect, I hit a poor shot, leading to a double bogey. That day, I learned some valuable lessons that I pass on to all my students: first, the importance of proper hydration before, during and after a round of golf. I also gained a new perspective of the value of a caddie – someone to calm a nervous soul, confirm a number and point a lost player in the right direction under the pressures of tournament golf.

I often think of this story and relate it to my journey in life. So often, life has a way of beating me down. It could be divorce, work, living situation, debt or simply being stuck in traffic. Wouldn't it be nice to be able to give our problems to someone else, feel internal peace and not worry about the outcome? I have often said that one of the biggest advantages and greatest assets tour players have is their caddie. Tour players play under tremendous pressure, and no matter how seasoned a player, the pressure sometimes is overwhelming. The faithful caddie is a confidant, a valuable member of the team, who is more than someone who carries a bag for a living. This faithful servant is often a rock of encouragement a player leans on during a difficult day on the course or a calming presence when the player is about to win a championship. I needed such a presence in my life many years ago on that hot, summer day.

I now have such a caddie leading my life journey. His name is Jesus Christ. The scriptures say it best: ***"Cast your burdens on the Lord, and He shall sustain you" (Psalm 55:22).*** Sometimes the Lord asks me to do my part, my chosen work, but He never leaves my side. In the game of life, choosing to go it alone or rely solely on our own resources or talents can be a dangerous proposition. We all need guidance on our daily walk; we were not designed to go it alone. Seek and choose the Lord to be your faithful servant, to share the journey. Follow His lead, trust His number and rest in His comfort. You will find this decision to be the most important shot of your life!

Golf Tips Magazine March/April 2021 Issue

Chapter 10

The Long Wait

"Be still, and know that I am God." (Psalm 46:10)

During the summer of 2003, I qualified for the Florida Open after shooting 72 on Rolling Oaks Golf Course at World Woods in Brooksville, Florida. The state open that year was being held in South Florida on two fantastic golf courses, Loblolly Pines and Sailfish Point Country Club. A few weeks prior to the tournament, I made a separate trip from Orlando south to get in an extra practice round. I also increased my training time, hitting balls for hours a day in the Florida heat as well as refining my touch around the greens. I was ready both physically and mentally and confident for the challenge ahead.

The four-day tournament was played on the two venues with a 36-hole cut. My first round was at Loblolly. I remember my warm-up session vividly. I literally did not miss a shot, and the confidence that was growing in my mind began to wrestle with the nervousness in the pit of my stomach. The first hole is a short par 4. During the early 2000s, I had a 3-wood that was literally my best friend. I could hit it between 260 and 270 yards off the tee and consistently much straighter than my driver, which loved to go 300 yards, but not always straight. The first tee nerves along with the hole layout called for the 3-wood, but I must admit that my swing felt slightly different standing on the tee box than what I had remembered from the driving range. I did get the opening tee shot into play, but I found the heavy rough, certainly not my best. I did manage to dig my approach shot out from the thick rough onto the front of the green and walked away with a two-putt par. Normally my nerves after playing the first hole are but a vast memory, but not that day. The accelerated walk with my caddie to the next hole led to an unexpected wait, and the teacher in me started taking over. "What happened to the swing that was on the driving range," I thought to myself. After a wait of more than 10 minutes on the par-3 second hole and a quick swing critique, I hit a horrible iron shot and made double bogey. I then followed up with another bogey, and my preround confidence had turned into a mental golf clinic with yours truly as both student and coach. I was now 3 over par.

It was time for the player in my split personality to step up to the plate. I forgot about my swing and started focusing on my target. Next hole…birdie! Then a few pars and then another birdie, and I made the turn at 1 over. On number 10, I hit a beautiful iron shot and made another birdie, and suddenly I was back to even par. I was now on my second life and my entire mind-set had changed. I was ready to go low, plus I had two birdie holes ahead! The first one was a reachable par 5, which was immediately followed by a drivable par 4. But, as my caddie and I approached the number 12 tee box, we saw an unexpected site — a sea of humanity. I counted five groups of players ahead of our group, plus their caddies, all waiting to tee off. The players were forced to wait because most of the field was going for both greens (the par 5 in two shots and the par 4 in one) trying to make eagle, forcing all groups to wait for the players to clear the green. This unusual situation created a massive logjam, the likes of which I had never seen. The wait on both holes took almost an hour. It was during this time that my true personality as both a player and man became transparent, revealing one of my greatest weaknesses. That day the game of golf exposed a chink in my armor, one that would not be addressed until years later, through the agony of time spent during the long wait.

As an adult who has started the back nine of my life, I have finally come to the realization that I am not a patient person. So, a few years ago I made a conscious decision to pray about my weakness and asked God for help in this area. They say in life, "Be careful what you ask for." I now understand that quote completely. God began immediately testing me. No matter what I did in my career, my personal relationships or living situations, God made me wait. The Bible is full of stories where God asked His children to wait. I love reading stories from the Bible about others waiting for God's promise to come to fruition, but I wanted no part of that test in my life. I wanted God to do the work overnight so that I could receive my rewards now!

In the Bible, God prepared Moses for 40 years as a shepherd. His preparation for Moses was not in vain or a punishment or his lot in life. God used this preparatory time to refine Moses as well as teach him to be a leader. God tested Moses' patience. One of the greatest lessons I have learned through my personal long wait is that it's not the amount of time God makes you wait that matters; it's the attitude we wait with that is the key to passing His test. I now wait in expectation for the Lord. During the Florida Open, I waited as a golf teacher, I got upset and waited in frustration because I had prepared as a player but had not factored in a one-hour wait. I failed the test that day.

I now pray into the future. I thank God for answering my prayers before they have been answered, because I know that in the future He will, even if the answer is not what I want to hear. I also know that Jesus is like a faithful caddie, standing right by my side, ready to listen. Sometimes in life, God answers our prayers by taking away the idols that we as humans often rely on (money, talent, success, etc.) so that we will be still, know that He is God and allow Him to lead. God knows my future. He is currently standing there, even as He stands with me today. So why would I not trust Him?

After the long wait, I parred the next two holes and shot 77, and the next day I shot 79 to miss the cut. Although I left South Florida disappointed, I learned a valuable lesson. I may not lead a nation in my lifetime from captivity like Moses or win the state open, but God does have a plan for me. If you are facing a long wait in your life, like a pandemic or financial hardship, remember that God is standing on your future and the long wait is no surprise to Him. In the end, the greatest lesson I learned from the long wait is that it is better to miss the cut than to miss an opportunity to stand still with the Lord, trust and know that my future is in His hands!

Golf Tips Magazine Jan/Feb 2021 Issue

CHAPTER 11

THE TRUNK SLAMMERS

"For it is by grace you have been saved, through faith—and this is not from yourselves, it is the gift of God not by works, so that no one can boast." (Ephesian 2:8-9)

In the summer of 2004, I was enjoying the fruits of my teaching labor. At the time, I was married, and my wife and I had spent several years building a new lakefront home in Oakland, Florida, a sleepy suburban town northwest of Orlando. The golf business was on fire, and the housing market was even hotter, allowing the two of us to dip into our equity and add a backyard swimming pool. Every day I would come home after a long day of teaching in the searing Florida heat and dive into the cool water to wash away the dust from a long day of lessons.

My game at the time was also in great shape, so I decided to use the new pool for more than a quick outdoor bath; it was now part of my afternoon workout program. I have never been much of a swimmer, even though I love the water, so I started swimming laps every day. Over time, my technique improved, I gained more stamina and increased my flexibility. "Who knows? Swimming laps may improve my golf swing," I thought to myself.

In August of that year, I signed up to play in the North Florida Section Championship at Innisbrook in Palm Harbor, Florida. The 54-hole event was to be played on the Copperhead Course where the Valspar Championship is currently played every spring during the Florida swing of the PGA TOUR. I was excited to play in the event and felt my game was ready for the test that lay ahead. In preparation for the tournament, I would go to work, hit balls and work on my short game between lessons and try to get in a quick nine whenever time permitted. I had to maximize every hour at work during the hottest months of the year. My afternoon workouts in the pool were a welcome sight and a highlight each day.

I signed up to play in the North Florida Section Championship as well as a Pro/Pro event the day prior to event with my work colleague Jason Bell. The Pro/Pro Tournament was a two-man, best-ball tournament held the day before the Section Championship. We all used the Pro/Pro as an opportunity to see the course, but it was still a tournament with prize money, making it more than just a practice round.

The day before departing to Palm Harbor, I packed my bags and prepared to leave bright and early for the two-hour drive. The next day, I awoke in the early morning with an earache. The pain was very severe, and I realized that for me to be able to play golf, I needed to go to urgent care prior to driving to Palm Harbor. Luckily, my tee time was in the afternoon, and I had time to stop on my way. The doctor confirmed my worst fears and said I had an ear infection (or "swimmers' ear") from all my late afternoon laps without ear plugs. He prescribed some oral antibiotics and told me to stay out of the sun. "Ok," I replied, as his advice went into my one good ear and out the bad ear on the other side. I got into my Toyota 4Runner and drove straight to Palm Harbor, knowing good and well that the next three days would feel like a living hell in 90-degree plus heat, with an ear infection while taking antibiotics.

I called Jason on my drive to Palm Harbor and told him the bad news. I was on my way but had no idea how I was going to play golf. When I arrived at Innisbrook, my earache had worsened. I played as hard as I could that day but was not much of a partner. As we signed our scorecard, I told the North Florida tournament director, Jerry Porter, that withdrawal was possible from the Section Championship if I didn't feel better overnight. I had never withdrawn from an event before, but under these circumstances, the possibility was very real.

The next morning, I awoke in my hotel room around 6 a.m. and my sheets were soaking wet. I had broken a fever and felt much better. Although I was not 100% and still had an ache in my right ear, I felt reenergized and made up my mind that I was not going to withdraw. I drove to the course ready to give it my best effort. For the next two days I played as hard as possible, even though my energy level was not at the same level as my desire. I shot 76 in the first round, certainly not my best, but considering how bad I felt, I knew in my heart it was about as well I as I could have expected. I was right there on the cut line and knew that I would need to play well the second round to make the cut.

The second day I was running on fumes. The heat, the antibiotics and the pain in my right ear, although better, was still there. I stood on the 18th hole at Copperhead, a demanding 445-yard uphill par 4. My drive found the right side of the fairway. I knew if I made birdie, I would make the cut and par would give me an outside chance. I hit a great approach shot with an 8-iron about 8 feet from the hole. I now faced a left-to-right uphill putt. I stood beside the ball making my practice swings, visualized the ball rolling into the cup and made my stroke. As I looked up, I was certain the ball was going to go into the right side of the cup, I was going to make birdie and make the cut on the number. However, as the ball rolled to the hole, it began to lose its speed, caught the right side of the hole and slowly lipped out.

I tapped in for par and a score of 74 knowing that my day was about to get much longer. Now began the long wait as I sat around the clubhouse for two hours to see if I was in for the final round. Would I be driving to my hotel to stay another night or was I heading back home tired and dejected? These were the questions running through my mind. After several hours of waiting, the news was not good. I missed the cut by one shot, walked to my car dejected with my head down, put the clubs in the back of my Toyota 4Runner and slammed the trunk with a little bit more authority than usual. Today I was a "trunk slammer." It was not the first time I had experienced this dubious title, but today it hurt even more because I knew in my heart I had given my best, with all that I had, and it still wasn't good enough.

Each week on the PGA TOUR and professional tours all around the world, half of the field entrants will be known as "trunk slammers" — players whose scores for the first 36 holes were not up to snuff and finished in the bottom half of the field. It is as if the tournament organizers say to the participants, "Thank you for coming, but your services are no longer required this week." It is a cruel business, especially for those who are so close, coming down to the last hole and the last putt only to come up one shot short.

My two-hour drive back home that day gave me time to digest the past three days and, believe me, it hurt. The "what ifs" started running through my mind about every shot over 36 holes that could have allowed me the opportunity to keep playing golf and cash a check. Now all I had to show for my efforts were receipts for my bills in the form of hotel, gas and food, not to mention lost work revenue from time away. The time spent in the car that late afternoon exposed the harsh realities professional golfers face weekly, realities not seen when the Masters Champion puts on the green jacket or the winning player kisses the Claret Jug. All professional golfers, even the greatest players in the world, on any given week experience the pain and frustration of missing the cut.

In the game of life, there are days when I feel like a "trunk slammer." Some days, life has a way of letting me know, "Jon, you're not good enough." It could be the score on my card, a student who decides to go to another teacher or a social media post where someone's life seems to be better off than mine. We all experience an inferiority complex at times in life when we compare someone else's career, success, money or lifestyle to our own. I have fallen into this trap very often during my lifetime. I have learned from personal reflection, when the world was telling me that I was a trunk slammer, to not believe the lies from the enemy. Now, when I come up short in life, I look at it not as a failure but as a growth opportunity.

I never realized that my experience as a trunk slammer would lead to God giving me this article to write decades later. I also use my experience to teach my students about the inevitable failures they will experience with the game of golf. I have grown to love my failed experiences because in every one of them I learned something about myself as a player, as a Christian and as a man. I also use these experiences when teaching to motivate my students to reflect, learn and then work to improve their weaknesses in their own game. Being a trunk slammer is not a failure but an opportunity to reflect and then improve. This opportunity starts with a conscious decision to first not give up, followed by a thirst, a desire and the effort to put in the necessary work.

But, when it comes to life and the standard set by God, the Bible and Ten Commandments, we have all failed to make the cut. But there is good news: God loves all the trunk slammers of the world! My faith journey has taught me one major difference between Christianity and golf. In golf, you must work to improve no matter how much talent you possess. However, Christianity is much different because God loves you no matter how much you have failed, through His grace. I made the mistake for years thinking that I needed to earn God's love through effort and hard work, like I did when I finally fixed my childhood slice. Then one day while studying Ephesians, I realized that you cannot work your way into Heaven. It is important to use our God-given abilities, for example, to give to the poor or volunteer at a homeless shelter, but that work and effort is not why God loves us. God's grace is a gift that flows freely to all His children, to us from Him. Our responsibility is to ask for forgiveness when we fall short, worship Him and receive His grace. Through God's grace, we are now saved to do good works, to fulfill our God-given purpose and to make this planet a much better place for all.

Golf Tips Magazine Nov/Dec 2022 Issue

CHAPTER 12

THE BALANCED FINISH:
OUT WITH THE OLD AND IN WITH THE NEW

"And no one puts new wine into old wineskins; if he does, the wine will burst the skins, and the wine is lost, and so are the skins; but new wine is for fresh skins." (Mark 2:22)

There is nothing like playing golf with a student on a beautiful summer morning, just before the rush of golfers leave the driving range to catch their morning tee time. To seek the quiet space on the course, I often take my students a few holes ahead of the first tee, fleeing from the crowd to come. To be the first group out is like stepping onto virgin soil as we approach each green and test the greenskeeper's new pin placements for the day. The freshly cut greens are like an oasis, always receptive after the dew has been swept away and just before the mid-morning sun rises above the tallest trees. The playing lesson is one of my favorite ways to not only teach the game but also to measure and gauge a student's improvement over the long haul.

Playing lessons can be challenging for some students because their safety net, the driving range, has been taken away. During playing lessons, the golf course is where the old habits of the past meet the new skills learned from previous lessons. It is where new and unexpected situations occur — ones that have not been covered in prior lessons. As a teaching professional, it is my job to harness the technical lingo that often accompanies a lesson on the range. On the course, my job is to evaluate students' strengths and weaknesses and help them navigate the hazards that blanket the course, all the while, keeping a watchful eye on the pace of play. Oh, and by the way, I am expected to play at a high level as well. Over my career, I have learned to juggle the many aspects of the playing lesson and boil it down to a simple mantra for my students: Pick your target and swing to a balanced finish.

I recall watching a CBS broadcast during a PGA Tournament telecast when former Masters and British Open Champion Sir Nick Faldo said, "When I played tournament golf, my only swing thought was to turn toward the target to a balanced finish." When I heard Faldo utter those words, I was somewhat amazed. Faldo was known for being an extremely technical player, always refining and dissecting his golf swing technically in his mind. Faldo worked under David Ledbetter, a teacher known for his technical understanding of the golf swing. Their marriage as both teacher and coach worked well for them because, in many ways, they thought alike. There is no doubt that working on your golf swing through the trained eye of a teaching professional, spending hours a day refining your swing and honing your short game will improve your game. The key to this marriage of old habits (your instincts) and new skills (lessons from your mentor) is a balancing act that all golfers face once they step off the driving range and onto the first tee box. Ultimately for this marriage of old and new to work, the old ways must fade away and the new ways must come to the forefront of the subconscious mind, to shine through when the pressure is on the line.

In 2008, I started working with Bob Sowards while he was playing on the PGA TOUR. We started working in May during the week of the Memorial Tournament at Muirfield Village Golf Club in Columbus, Ohio. With only a few days of work under my belt as his full-time golf coach, we dove right in and began working on his ball position, quick transition and knee drive during his downswing. I knew I could help him, but I also knew it was not going to be a quick fix. Bob was going to have to trust me and the changes that needed to be made. This process was not going to happen overnight. He missed the cut that week and the following week at the St. Jude Classic in Memphis, Tennessee. I worried that Bob might revert to his old ways and abandon his new swing of only a few weeks. We worked together every day that summer and, by August, Bob was playing some of the best golf of his life. This success included a ninth-place finish at the Wyndham Championship in Greensboro, North Carolina, and a final round back nine score of 28 at the Valero Texas Open to finish tied for 19th. I told Bob later that year that he would be working on these changes for the rest of his life. I said, "Swing flaws are like being an alcoholic. Alcoholics can stop drinking but they are still an alcoholic. They must consciously stay away from old situations that would cause them to want to start drinking again. You can't be a recovering alcoholic and continue to go back to your old ways." In golf, you need to know your weaknesses, not by thinking negatively but by being aware of your old ways, so when they show up on the golf course, your focus shifts back to the new way. This balancing act of the old swing verses the new swing ultimately becomes a mental hurdle that every player faces during the learning journey. This process can be uncomfortable at first but necessary, until the new ways become engrained in the subconscious mind, like tying your shoes or logging onto your computer. The learning process takes thousands of hours and must be practiced daily before trust is developed. The "out with the old and in with the new" song and dance is not needed only for the golf course but is also necessary in orchestrating the harmony of life as well.

As a member of the PGA since 1997, I have noticed a trend in the message being delivered to its nearly 29,000 members. The term "work-life balance" comes up in every meeting I attend or newsletter I read. I applaud our organizational effort to highlight this problem. I love being a PGA member, but frankly, the golf business can be brutal at times, especially during high season. Every PGA member has a high season, and during this time, golf professionals are working six to seven days a week, often sunup to sundown. I highlighted this work-life balance in my first book. In the book, I confessed that I am a recovering workaholic. During my 30s and 40s, I rarely said "no" to any lesson request. I would cut lunches short, stayed longer at work than was expected, worked every weekend and abandoned my church. I literally ran myself into the ground standing on the lesson tee. I stopped playing competitive golf or even a casual round with friends. My logic was simple: If I am going to be outside on the course, I wanted to be making money. As you might expect, this lifestyle led to burnout and a divorce. Now years later, I have new priorities in life. I now take Sundays off, winter in Florida to escape the cold Ohio winter and slow down, allowing more time to exercise, read, write, work on my own game, play in section tournaments and enjoy life. This balanced time away from teaching has made me a better teacher because I am able to bring more energy and passion to every lesson I teach and, at the end of the day, spend more time with those I love. I have finally started to learn that by letting go of my old ways, I've allowed new opportunities to come into my life.

In December of 2020, I met Carla on a blind date that was set up by my cousin Janelle. Our first date was during the pandemic, so going out to a restaurant was out of the question. Carla agreed to cook dinner for Janelle, her husband, Steve, and me at her beautiful house. "What do I have to lose?" I thought to myself as the three of us drove to Carla's home. That night I would be introduced to the woman I would later ask to marry, but I was also introduced to something more: a new lifestyle change. Carla had adopted a whole food plant-based diet without oil. I knew early on that I liked Carla and really had no problem giving up the old comfort foods that I loved such as meats, dairy and certain desserts. The new dietary lifestyle introduced to me included foods that I already loved, including fruits and vegetables, beans, whole grain pasta, brown rice, potatoes of all kinds as well as some breads.

Over the last 10 years, I have been dealing with psoriasis. My dermatologist treated my psoriasis with steroid creams, which have not helped. Fast forward to January of 2023. Now engaged, Carla and I attended a five-day supervised water fast at the Balance for Life Health Retreat in Deerfield Beach, Florida. The event was hosted by Dr. Frank Sabatino. Prior to attending, we were required to submit a blood test to be approved for the water fast. Our class included 20 people from all over the world. I realized early on that the supervised water fast was more psychological than physical. After day one, I woke up dreaming I was eating sweet potatoes. When I opened my eyes, I realized my mouth was chewing imaginary food. On days two and three, I realized how many pizza commercials were on TV while watching the NFL playoffs, and by day four, I realized there was no degree of hungriness. The hunger you feel on day one is the same as day four. During the supervised fast, we attended lectures and were monitored by Dr. Frank twice a day. He checked our pulse, blood pressure and weight and instructed us to drink plenty of water and to rest. The idea for the fast is to starve the old cells and detox the organs while flushing toxins out of the body. This process allows for new healthy cells to grow. According to Dr. Frank, water fasting has reversed heart disease and cured numerous auto-immune diseases — even cancer. As for my psoriasis, I saw amazing results to the point where my psoriasis was almost gone after several weeks. What I learned most was that God created our bodies to heal themselves. By getting rid of the poisons from my old diet and adopting a new dietary lifestyle, my body was able to work the way God intended, which allowed the healing process to begin.

Whether learning to take your swing from the driving range to the golf course, juggling your work-life schedule, finding time to exercise or spending time with the family, life is a constant balancing act. In ***Mark 2:18-22***, the people asked Jesus, ***"Why do John's disciples and the disciples of the Pharisees fast, but your disciples do not?"*** Jesus responded with three parables. The third parable was about the wineskins. In Jesus' day, new wine was put into new wineskins. When you put grape juice into a wineskin, it would ferment. As the juice fermented, the wineskin would expand. If you put new wine into an old wineskin, as the juice fermented, the old wineskin would burst and the wine would be lost. Getting rid of the old wineskins and using new wineskins was a necessary step in making new wine.

In the parable, Jesus was stating that at that time fasting was not needed by His disciples because He was with them. Jesus was the "new way." The disciples needed to focus on the new way, the Messiah, standing in front of them, not the old ways, i.e., laws of the past. There would be time in the future for the disciples to fast, but not now. Jesus' parable of the wineskins reminds us that in order to have a balance of the Old Testament with the New Testament, you must balance the old laws with the new way, Jesus Christ. Jesus healed the sick, raised the dead and came to this Earth to be the sacrificial lamb for all our sins.

The balanced finish of life is not a destination but a journey. God does not ask us to be perfect but to lay down or let go of anything that keeps us from Him and to simply take the next step forward. Things I once thought to be important are now distant memories. The Bible often refers to the old habits or desires as "the flesh." The battle between the flesh and our soul is something every human being faces during his/her journey. In golf, the flesh is our old, engrained flawed habits that have been with us for years. Letting go of the old ways often takes guidance through instruction. Once taught, it takes commitment, hard work and patience to see the old self fade away before the new and better version can come shining through. Life and faith follow the same recipe. Looking back at my first date with Carla when I asked myself what I had to lose, it turned out to be 35 pounds, inflammation and psoriasis. But that night was so much more as I ushered in a new way of living and let go of the old ways, changing my life forever and leading me to the woman I will one day call my wife.

Golf Tips Magazine May/June 2023 Issue

CHAPTER 13

THE DREAM FOURSOME

"But you shall receive power when the Holy Spirit has come upon you; and you shall be witnesses to Me in Jerusalem, and in all Judea and Samaria, and to the end of the Earth." (Acts 1:8)

In the fall of 2016, my first book was released, giving birth to a new and exciting chapter for my life. Following the book's release, I began an eight-month book tour, traveling more than 20,000 miles by car across eight states. The tour included numerous book signings and newspaper, radio and podcast interviews, as well as public speaking engagements at churches, book clubs and civic organizations. I was no longer standing on the familiar grounds of the lesson tee but now swimming in uncharted waters as a first-time author. This eight-month hiatus had no guaranteed income or audience. To say that I was not scared would be a lie, but I will admit there was a side of me that welcomed the new and exciting challenge. Instead of counting one shot at a time on the golf course, I was now literally peddling one book at a time to whoever cared to listen.

Years before moving to Ohio to become the director of instruction at the Medallion Club, I was teaching at the Grand Cypress Academy of Golf in Orlando, Florida, where I met Rob Walgate. Rob, along with Alan C. Duncan, co-hosted a podcast called *The Pine*. The studio resided in Strongsville, Ohio, a town just south of Cleveland. Although I had never given Rob lessons personally, I got to know him very well while he took winter golf trips to Florida to escape the bitter cold of the North. We connected on social media and, years later when I decided to write my first book, I reached out to him to see if my book and story would be of interest for his show. Rob agreed to have me on his podcast as a guest and allowed an unknown author the opportunity to market and promote his Christian book. *The Pine* podcast is about sports and faith, a perfect fit for my Christian book about golf, sports, life and Jesus. It was the opportunity I had prayed for, and God answered.

I was on cloud nine as I made the hour-and-a-half drive north up Interstate-71 to the studio. Early into the marketing process, I had done several newspaper, radio and podcast interviews over the phone but never in studio. I was a bit nervous but also knew beforehand that the interview would be recorded and edited, so any mistakes would be erased. The interview was graced with a mulligan if needed, unlike the shots of tournament golf where everything counts. I remember how I felt driving to the studio that day. I thought about the questions that might be asked, how I would respond and what stories I wanted to highlight from the book. It was like I was playing in a golf tournament and visualizing every shot and every hole as I dissected the course in my mind. However, these plans were often short-lived as mistakes, misfortune and the unpredictable conditions on the course inevitably forced my mind to go back to the drawing board time after time.

I met Rob and Alan at the studio. After a quick tour of the facility, we sat down to discuss the interview. The three of us were seated around a large, round wooden table inside a glass walled room. I felt as though I was living inside a fishbowl where others could see but not hear me through the soundproof walls. In front of me and the other hosts were large adjustable microphones that were carefully positioned inches away from our faces. Behind the glass in a separate room was the director who orchestrated the show. I remember saying a short prayer to myself seconds before the interview started and asking the Holy Spirit to take over my thoughts and words. As the director gave us the cue that we were now recording, our conversation began to flow, like old friends sitting around a warm campfire rehashing stories from yesteryear.

At first the questions were familiar and predictable. We talked about my career path as a PGA teaching professional, why I had decided to take on the task of writing the book and some of my favorite stories. Prior to the interview, Rob had read the book, so as the conversation progressed the questions became more specific. Rob carefully crafted questions and went away from the plans of dialogue I had formed in my mind while driving north earlier that day. But with each question they asked, my confidence grew as I felt more and more at ease in my new surroundings.

The time sitting in the leather chair behind the microphone flew by in an instant. The next thing I knew, we were wrapping up the hour, but there was one more bow for the present. Rob unexpectedly said to me, "Jon, I ask these final two questions to all my guests. If you could play any golf course in the world, which one would you play?" Without hesitation I responded, "Augusta." "That was an easy one," I thought to myself. Then Rob delivered a curveball. "What would be your dream foursome when you played Augusta?" I was stumped by Rob's question. I had never thought of that question in my life, and silence filled the room. I'm sure to Rob and Alan the silence was temporary, but to me it felt like an eternity. Suddenly, like a favorable kick from the trees on an errant tee shot, my ball landed safely onto the fairway, as the Holy Spirit stepped into the conversation.

Although my mind had no response to Rob's question, my lips began to unexpectedly move. I answered, "I would have my dad...," paused several seconds then continued... "I would have Jack Nicklaus...," paused again and while still thinking Rob chimed in, "Remember who invited you here to the show today?" I nervously laughed at his remark, but my mind was blank. Suddenly, the Holy Spirit spoke to me, and I said without hesitation, "I would have Jesus. That would be my foursome." The room immediately filled with chatter, and everyone started adding in their perspective about having Jesus in my dream foursome. It was the perfect fit for me!

First, my childhood hero, my dad, a 10-handicap player at best who fearlessly attempts shots like his hero, Arnold Palmer, but unfortunately does not receive Palmer-like results. My second member would be my lifetime golfing hero, Jack Nicklaus, winner of 18 major championships. The last player, but certainly not the least member of my dream foursome, would be my Lord and Savior, Jesus Christ. Without hesitation, the Holy Spirit once again chimed in and the following words came rolling off my tongue, adding the perfect ending to this amazing experience. I responded, "The problem is my father would try to tell Jesus how to play golf!" At that moment, the entire room burst into spontaneous laughter!

I often reflect with a smile on my face about that day and interview when thinking about my journey. I now have a new dream foursome, not for the golf course but for my daily life. First is God, my heavenly Father, maker of Heaven and Earth. Second is Jesus Christ, the sacrificial lamb who died for my sins. The third member is the Holy Spirit, God Himself, living inside of me, speaking to my mind and heart every step of the way as I walk through this dark and troubled world. I received the gift of the Holy Spirit when I received Jesus Christ as my Lord and Savior. The last member of this foursome is me, a flawed, selfish, sinful man who is certainly the highest handicapper in the group. My foursome is not about hitting perfect golf shots or setting a new course record. My foursome is about daily life experiences, daily choices and, most importantly, being a follower and trying my best not to be the leader of the group. I have learned that by following the Word of God, following Jesus' life examples and listening to the Holy Spirit, I make better choices and decisions. Through these experiences, I am slowly becoming a better version of the man God created me to be.

The greatest lesson I learned while attempting to write my first book was listening to the Holy Spirit. As part of my book tour, I had the opportunity to speak to thousands of people. I talked about my fear of writing and the four-year struggle of getting my book published. I never wanted to write a book but knew God was asking me to do so. One day, I found the secret to improved writing and completing this monumental task I had once deemed impossible. I simply prayed to God and asked Him to give me the words and show me the way, and then followed. For the first time in my life, I truly understood what the Holy Spirit was. God Almighty living inside of me, giving me what I needed at that moment. What He gave me wasn't always what I expected, but looking back, it was always what I needed and always enough.

I always finish my speeches by talking about my childhood dreams. I say the following: "My dream was to be a PGA TOUR player and to win the Masters. I am so thankful that my dreams did not come true. If I had won the Masters, I would have thanked my coaches, my parents and my sponsors. I would not have thanked God, Jesus nor the Holy Spirit. I would have thought that my efforts and hard work were why I won." I then hold up my book and conclude: "I have to thank God for this book. I never wanted to write a book, but I knew He was asking me to do it. I have to thank God for giving me the words, because without Him, I couldn't have written one word. To God I give the glory!" Looking back at my writing experience and how the Holy Spirit led me, I now have a much better understanding of what Jesus spoke in Act 1:8. Ask, listen, follow and who knows? Your journey may take you to the ends of the earth!

To listen to Jon's entire interview online search "The Pine Jon Decker"

Golf Tips Magazine March/April 2023 Issue

As Seen Through My Eyes

by

Kraig Kann

Former Network Broadcaster and Founder of Kann Advisory
Group

In the professional world, there are many careers from which we can choose, many paths we can take and many pivots we'll make along the way. Not every career is a straight road. And, as I have told many people along my own journey, to be our very best unique self, we need to set the curve, not follow the curve. In golf terms, that means going for the green when others might lay up and play it safe.

I've known Jon for a number of years, all tied to an original link to the game of golf. I was a lead anchor at NBC's Golf Channel and played much of my golf at the Grand Cypress Academy of Golf in Orlando, Florida, where Jon was a head instructor.

Our paths moved in different directions. I eventually left a longtime television career to be an executive with the Ladies Professional Golf Association (LPGA) and then pivoted completely by starting Kann Advisory Group. As a consultant "elevating communication" for leaders in the corporate space, I now travel as a keynote speaker and lead workshops for teams and individuals to help transform employees into ambassadors and storytellers of their brand.

Jon came to me with a clear purpose. He wanted to elevate his own game and take the steps to build a brand worth following.

In my workshops, I share my years of experience as a presenter and help people to dig deep and find the value in their story, and I then help them learn to present the best of themselves and also the best of their organization. For Jon, this was a chance to clarify his message and learn to dynamically present it in ways he wasn't comfortable doing. This time, he wasn't helping others to become better at something. He was laser-focused on helping himself.

Jon invested two days going through my program *A Brand New You.* And just like the many executives finding their way through this immersive and experiential workshop, Jon learned not just who he was but who he wants others to see. He learned the difference between "giving a talk" and "delivering an experience."

In truth, I challenged Jon for being so focused on faith. Like Jon, I, too, have religion in my life. But putting it out there isn't always easy to deliver, and it's not always well-received. But Jon is different. Just like the impact he makes as a leading golf instructor in the industry, he has a unique ability to make people comfortable with things that are uncomfortable. For Jon, faith and religion fit his brand. The challenge I posed to him during our work together actually ties to the sport we both love.

In golf, we start with the right grip, learn to address the ball properly, take aim at the target and swing away with confidence that the ball lands just right.

In presenting his brand, Jon needed to get a firm grip on what his message actually was. I wanted to make sure he addressed his audience properly, knowing who he wanted to inspire and empower. And then I wanted to coach him on how to "swing away" and deliver the best of himself.

In my experience, many people talk but very few actually have something to say. I wanted to make sure that Jon's message wasn't lost among the many speakers out there. Together, we worked to transform Jon Decker the person into Jon Decker "the experience."

I'm proud to call Jon a friend. And I think this book is proof that brands are always under construction. They evolve. And the more we share, the bigger they can become.

Jon's got plenty of fairway left. I'm excited to see the back nine score he posts and all the great shots he delivers along the way.

Like the green tennis shoe, Kraig's workshop inspired me to "stand out" in all that I do. I was honored to receive one!

Chapter 14

The Narrow Fairway

"Enter by the narrow gate; for wide is the gate and broad is the way that leads to destruction, and there are many who go in by it. Because narrow is the gate and difficult is the way which leads to life, and there are few who find it." (Matthew 7:13-14)

In January of 2022, I made a financial decision to invest in myself. Although my career has evolved over the years from a full-time PGA teaching professional to a part-time author and public speaker, I knew in my heart God was asking me to stretch myself and grow professionally. My career path has certainly been unexpected. My childhood dream was to be a PGA TOUR player, and nothing was going to stop me! Looking back on those early years of childhood exuberance, I realize my plans were not led by God and don't recall asking Him for help or His desire for my life. Now as an adult who has started the back nine of my life, I have different dreams and have learned to turn them over to my Creator and ask one simple question: "What is your will, Father?"

God has given me natural talents for certain skills that were apparent to me from childhood, such as people skills or athletic ability. However, some skills were not so apparent and took decades to develop. Never once as a high school or college student did a teacher or professor come up to me and say, "Jon you have a natural talent for writing. You should write a book." These skills didn't become apparent to me until I was in my early 40s and had recommitted my life back to the Lord and asked Him to lead.

I learned this valuable life lesson when I wrote my first book, a difficult labor of love that stretched me out of my comfort zone and forced me not to rely on my myself but the strength of the Lord. This writing journey took more than four years to birth. After the book was released, I knew God was asking me to stretch my faith again to be a public speaker and to spread His Word, but I didn't know where to start. I knew I needed a mentor. I also knew deep down in my heart that God was asking me to seek earthly help and that not all the guidance was going to come directly from Him. God was asking me to seek an old friend, Golf Channel's former lead studio host, Kraig Kann.

I met Kraig years ago from my stint as a head instructor at the Grand Cypress Academy of Golf. At the time, Kraig was studio host and on-air personality for the Golf Channel. I gave his teenage son, Trent, several lessons, and over time, a unique friendship was born. Kraig and I were about the same age, often played golf together, loved college football and were both dreamers.

In 2011, Kraig left the Golf Channel to be the chief communications officer for the LPGA and in 2016 formed his own company, Kann Advisory Group. Kraig's specialty is helping people learn to "stand out" whether as a keynote speaker in front of a large audience or as a management executive leading a small team or large company. I knew Kraig could help me, so through prayer and a lot of thought, I decided to make the investment to participate in his two-day boot camp with one-on-one instruction. I will never forget one of my early conversations with Kraig over the phone as I contemplated whether seeking his advice was the best thing for my career. Kraig asked me what I was trying to do in growing my brand, DeckerGolf. I replied, "I want to use the game of golf to grow Christianity." I will never forget Kraig's response: "Jon, I have seen your instructional videos and like what you are doing, but once you add the faith element, you are going down a very narrow road." I knew at that very moment that I wanted to follow Kraig's lead, commit to the narrow gate and follow the narrow road.

In the game of golf, the narrow gate is the target and the narrow road is the fairway. Sometimes the fairway is inviting and open and looks like an oasis. Other fairways are tight, treacherous and littered with bunkers, trees and water. "Never complain when you are in the fairway," is one of the many catchphrases to my students on the course when they are not satisfied with their drive that is not 300 yards down the middle. Choosing a target (or gate) is a critical first step in accomplishing that goal, and any attempt to go against the architect's design for the hole is risky. This includes aggressive strategies to go over tall trees or large bodies of water to shorten a hole. Missing the fairway through poor alignment, poor course management, unlucky bounces or simply a bad swing with the driver are the most common reasons why golfers post high scores.

These examples of the fairway design, contours, target strategies and course conditions are reasons why I fell in love with the game as a child. Each tee box, fairway and hole design in golf is different, unlike tennis or basketball, two other sports I grew up playing. In those sports, the dimensions of the playing field are the same. Although they were fun childhood activities, my first love was golf, and I couldn't wait to go to a new course. I looked at each hole as a new and exciting adventure.

To conquer these unique conditions on the course, the player must stand on the tee box and commit to a primary target or "choose a gate." There is an old story I heard years ago when Lee Trevino was playing in a charity outing with a local caddy. Lee had never played the course, and the hole was a blind shot over a rolling hill. The caddy confidently announced to Lee as they walked to the tee box, "Now on this hole, there is out of bounds on the left side, so stay right." Lee turned and looked at him and said, "Don't tell me where not to go. Show me the target and tell me where you want me to hit it." Trevino's comments illustrate why he was one of the greatest players to ever play the game. His comments may seem elementary to the average golfer but illustrate how brilliant his mind worked by highlighting Trevino's focus. Trevino chose to focus on the narrow gate that was down the right side of the fairway. He eliminated the distractions of the out of bounds from the wide gate on the left side.

In Christianity, the narrow gate (or target) and road is Jesus Christ. Choosing this road first starts with a conscious decision to enter the narrow gate. As stated in Matthew, the gate and road are difficult and followed by few. This commitment to stay on the road takes focus and, like the bunkers, trees and water that are distractions surrounding the narrow fairway, the narrow road of my life also has similar distractions. I am a planner, a dreamer and never seem to be satisfied with being average. As the saying goes, "No moss grows under my feet." Making a choice to follow Kraig's advice led me through the narrow gate. I then followed the road by making a financial commitment and doing the work that was not easy but worth it. This commitment and work on the narrow road stretched me to become a new and better version of myself. I know this investment will change how the world sees me through my golf instruction, videos, my website DeckerGolf.com, future books and speaking engagements. Time is short and the road less traveled can be lonely at times, but the reward is great. There is much work to do.

However, rushing through life and not waiting on the Lord to show me the direction to take for my next step can lead to disaster. The narrow road is tight! The world is full of distractions and, unfortunately, sin is one of my playing partners. But there is good news! I have chosen a third playing partner and so can you — a Savior, Jesus Christ. Each day, I can choose to focus on the world and be tempted by its sin on the wide and open road, or I can stretch myself, focus on the Lord and choose the narrow road. Although I know that the world will leave me if I choose the narrow road, I am truly never alone. I no longer worry about how others see me as a man because the wide road is blurred by the distractions of the world. Like a perfect drive on a well-bunkered fairway with water in front of the green, my ball has found the short grass. I walk confidently with my Savior to my ball, focusing on the shot ahead, looking past the distractions of the water and finding reassurance that He is with me. There is room on the narrow road, so choose your gate wisely, make the commitment, do the work and never walk alone.

Golf Tips Magazine Jan/Feb 2023 Issue

AS SEEN THROUGH MY EYES

by

Clark Kellogg

CBS College Basketball Analyst

Former NBA Player (1982-86), NBA All-Rookie Team (1982)

"The heavens declare the glory of God; the skies proclaim the work of his hands. Day after day they pour forth speech; night after night they display knowledge. There is no speech or language where their voice is not heard..." (Psalm 19:1-2)

I recite this Bible verse frequently, audibly and silently in my heart. The beauty, mystery and vastness of God's creation are awe-inducing, inspiring and humbling. And ever since bowing my heart and surrendering my life to God through faith in Jesus Christ in late 1986, an attitude of gratitude and a posture of praise for my new life in Him compels me to acknowledge and proclaim His glory and goodness earnestly and often. Made in the image of God according to His Word, I'm to reflect His image in the world – loving obeying, serving and trusting God by loving and serving others. It is both my aspiration and God-ordained mission to do so.

Less than a year after becoming a Christian, the "golf bug" grabbed me, and I continue to grab back. Afforded modest celebrity status as an NBA player, I often received invitations to participate in charity golf outings as a celebrity. Because I didn't play golf, I always declined. However, the combination of some of my NBA peers taking up the game, it being a way to use my celebrity status to support worthy charitable efforts and my competitive curiosity led me to give it a try.

The well-known golf club manufacturer Ping offered NBA players custom clubs at a nice discount back in the day, so I took advantage of this blessed perk. It was late spring 1987 when I got my first clubs. With an NBA players' trip to Hawaii planned for July, I took a couple of lessons at a local golf course in Indianapolis. Several players would be taking their clubs to Hawaii, so I was excited to do the same.

Armed with new clubs, a couple of lessons and great excitement, I was eager to experience my first 18 holes of golf! My maiden voyage on the links would take place at the renowned Kapalua Bay Course. Being a newbie to golf, I had NO idea how challenging and esteemed a venue Kapalua was for any player, not to mention a first-timer. I must have taken at least 200 swings dribbling my golf ball all over that course for close to five hours!! It was embarrassing and humbling. Yet despite the long day and after sleeping for 10 hours straight following my round, I was hooked! And I was also very grateful – for two things.

First, the more accomplished and experienced golfers that I played with patiently and graciously endured my ineptitude. No condemnation, frustration or judgment was spoken, at least not that I could discern or feel. Such grace and patience by them serve as a most memorable and forever model for me. Anytime I am paired with a beginning golfer, I treat them as I was treated by my peers back in the summer of 1987.

Second, I'm grateful for the gift that the game of golf has been to me for now approaching 40 years. The camaraderie it engenders with family and friends; the competition within and without; the universal challenges, experiences, frustrations, joys and sayings that are inherent to the game translate to life as well. The memories of matches lost and won; shots and scorecards that "make me smile in my sleep"; memorable trips with fellow golfers; and beautiful and majestic landscapes and layouts of fairways and greens where the game is played are gifts the game gives to all of us who play it in some measure.

One added note of gratitude goes to Jon, who I met in 2021 when he became the director of instruction at the Medallion Club. Jon has taken his love for God, golf and people and blended them together to inspire others through his life experiences playing and teaching the wonderful game of golf. His personal instruction has been helpful to my game, too.

"The heavens declare the glory of God; the skies proclaim the work of his hands. Day after day they pour forth speech; night after night they display knowledge. There is no speech or language where their voice is not heard."

I recite this verse frequently, audibly and silently in my heart. It makes me smile whenever and wherever I do. Especially on the golf course, on the first tee, where the gift of a round of golf has its start.

CHAPTER 15

THE COLOR OF THE GREEN

"So, God created man in His image; in the image of God, He created him, male and female. He created them. Then blessed them, and God said to them, 'Be fruitful and multiply.'"
(Genesis 1:27-28)

In golf, it could be argued that the color that best describes the game itself is the color green. The fairways and rough, if properly maintained, are green. The jacket awarded to the Masters Champion is green, and, of course, one of the objectives of the game is to hit fairways and, you guessed it, the green. In golf, the green is considered more than a color. It is a preferred destination as well as an equalizer, and, like snowflakes, no two are alike. The contours are uneven and the skill itself of mastering these surfaces is often taken for granted. The green is where numbers are calculated and, if the participants are honest and hole their last putt, is a place where players are judged only by a score. The green is a place of etiquette, a place where decorum and rules are not a wish but an expectation. When you first arrive at the green, it is a sin not to first take care of this hallowed ground. Repair the ball mark where your ball last hit and repair those who failed in their efforts. Pick up your feet, and never walk in someone's line. Ultimately, all golf courses are judged by this place, the smoother and faster the better, and their color better be green.

But when it comes to human beings, color should have no bearing at all, if you believe what is said in the Bible. God clearly states that "man was created in His image." For this reason, I dislike it when I hear terms like white, black, Hispanic, African American, minority or the hundreds of other man-made terms used to describe the color of a person's skin or origin in today's politically correct world. I often think to myself, "Does God think of me as a white male or a white American?" And what about the racial slurs, coming from both sides at times, that society has created to dehumanize others or, worse yet, use them for grounds to murder? I believe what the Bible says, and that means that when I look at someone else of a different color or religion, I try my best to recognize that they were created in the image of God.

It appears to me that the only race God considers important is the race He calls "the human race." God knows me by my first name. ***"Behold, I have engraved you on the palms of my hands; your walls are continually before me" (Isaiah 49:16).*** As far as our last names are concerned, in God's eyes mine is not Decker, but just like you it is "a child of God." With this understanding of how God sees me as a man, I must now investigate the often painful mirror of self-reflection. Two reflections are seen, one for the game that I love, while the other hits closer to home, revealing my actions as a human being over my lifetime. Both reflections before me require repentance by our society as well as my heart, and the time is now.

I love the game of golf, but with this love comes recognition of its faults. It is no secret that the game has discriminated against men and women for centuries. I am happy to say that there has been tremendous improvement in inclusion, job opportunities and memberships for both men and women around the world, but there is so much more work left to be done. In 2018, the PGA of America elected its first woman president, Suzy Whaley. High-profile clubs including Augusta National as well as other clubs known for discriminating in the past against people based on their race, religion or sex are now opening their memberships. Golf is being taught more in public schools as well as to low-income families and children through the First Tee Organization and other community organizations. Facilities all around the world are encouraging junior golf, a practice that was often frowned upon when I was a child. In 1977, the year I took up the game, there was no "Drive, Chip and Putt" competition with a trip to the Masters.

The subject of equality and inclusion in the game is so important to me that when I wrote my first book, I knew that I wanted my longtime friend, Pete McDaniel, to edit my book. If the government considers me to be a "Caucasian," then the government considers Pete to be an "African American." I wanted to write a chapter in my book called "Discrimination," and I wanted the chapter to tell an unfortunate story where I unknowingly used the N-word to a fellow classmate in grade school. I met with Pete in Atlanta for lunch and I told him, "Pete, I want you to be the editor for my book, but before you agree, I have to tell you about the chapter in the book titled 'Discrimination.'" Pete listened, passed no judgment and said to me, "Jon, you need to tell that story." When Pete echoed those words, I felt a sense of peace. I then asked Pete to write an introduction for that chapter describing discrimination, from his point of view, for the book. Pete agreed and provided an amazing picture of him and Tiger Woods together.

The chapter also talks about my first experience with golf and my introduction to the 17th hole, a 747-yard par-6, in my hometown of Black Mountain North Carolina. In 1977, hole 17 was listed by the *Guinness Book of World Records* as "The World's Longest Hole." After Pete edited the chapter, he said to me, "I love this chapter, Jon, but I would change one thing. I would change the title from 'Discrimination' to 'The World's Longest Hole.'" It was probably the single most important change we made in the book.

If our nation were a golf course, race relations would be "The World's Longest Hole." God did not declare that Adam be white or Eve be black because it was not an issue to God. God looks at us not by the outside but by our soul, which is encased in the temple we call the human body. No two bodies or souls are alike, and as the evolution of humanity continues, our colors as a society will begin to blend. I believe in my heart that the color that God ultimately has in mind for humanity will blend one day and be described as the color of Jesus Christ.

In my book, Pete so poetically wrote, *"If I live to be 100, I'll never understand man's inhumanity to other men."* We are all in this thing together. We are all on "The World's Longest Hole," and the green is there in front of us. It is a place where our society will ultimately be judged. But, as a society, including myself at times, we continue to take two-shot penalties. Violence toward each other and looting instead of peaceful protest, make "The World's Longest Hole" even longer. The good news is that "The World's Longest Hole" has an ending that has already been written: a place in Heaven where the greens are fast and pure, and the ball always finds the hole. Let us get to the green together as a human race by moving forward and loving one another. Let us get started today!

Chapter 16

Tribute to Roy

"Preach the word; be prepared in season and out of season; correct, rebuke and encourage with great patience and careful instruction." (2 Timothy 4:2).

On April 1, 2021, the legendary basketball coach for the University of North Carolina, Roy Williams, retired after 48 years of coaching. The man who led the Tar Heels to three national championships and 903 wins as a college basketball coach finally called it quits after 33 seasons. To the players who were fortunate enough to play for him, Roy was a teacher first, a man who brought enthusiasm, passion and dedication, along with a hard work ethic, to every team he coached. In most cases, his teams mirrored their leader.

I wrote a story about Roy Williams in 2016 in my first book. I never played for Roy, but the lessons I learned from him will last a lifetime. I think about Roy every time I teach the rules of golf. Why do I think about Roy? Because when I was a young teenage boy, chasing my dream to be a collegiate golfer and maybe one day a PGA TOUR player, Roy Williams took the time to teach me the rules of golf. I hope you enjoy this excerpt from the book.

"In the fall of 1983, I was paired with Roy Williams in the third and final round of the annual Labor Day Golf Tournament in Black Mountain, North Carolina. Roy grew up in the Asheville area and, after coaching at Charles D. Owen (the high school I graduated from), became an assistant coach under UNC legend Dean Smith. I was so excited when I saw my pairing in the final round. Roy and I had a great battle on the course. The conversations were entertaining and enlightening. Although I was extremely nervous to meet Roy for

the first time, he made me feel extremely comfortable. I started asking him questions about Michael Jordan, Sam Perkins and James Worthy. I am sure by the end of the round Roy was worn out with all my questions. On the last hole, I calmly made a 4-foot putt to shoot 74 and beat him by one stroke. Roy shook my hand and later told my parents how much he enjoyed playing with me. I was on cloud nine!

The next spring, our golf team won the Western North Carolina sectionals for the first time in school history, advancing to the state tournament in Chapel Hill. Roy and our coach, the late Ralph Singleton, were close friends. Roy came out and followed our team for two days. His presence inspired us to a fifth-place finish. After a first-round 74, I stood on the 36th and final hole 1-over-par for the day and was bursting with confidence. In fact, I laced a drive down the middle of the fairway and declared to my dad, "I'm going to get in the top 10." Classic mistake! I fatted my approach shot into the water fronting the 18th green. Roy and Coach Singleton were watching as I approached the lateral hazard. Suddenly, my nerves were so tingly I felt like a pin cushion. I dropped the ball in a sandy area and skulled my next shot over the green and under a tree. I was dead! I blindly chipped out from behind the tree and heard a funny thud. Fortunately, my ball had hit the flagstick and was 2 inches away from the cup. I anxiously walked up and tapped in for 6 as I looked for somewhere to hide. I learned an exceedingly difficult lesson that day about not staying in the moment and felt as though I had let the team down.

Roy calmly walked over and congratulated me on how well I had played for two days. He also took the time to explain the options of a lateral water hazard, which revealed that I had made an extremely poor decision in my drop and could have saved at least one stroke had I properly understood the rules of golf. When I teach the rules of golf to my students, I sometimes remind them of the many mistakes I have made in golf. Roy showed me patience and knowledge, but, more importantly, he gave me his time. For that, I can only say one thing: "Thank you, Roy!"

I will always remember that day because of Roy's generosity. I am sure he could tell by the disappointment on my face and the tears welling up in my eyes that I was hurting inside. Roy took a moment that was devastating in my mind and turned it into a teaching moment. From that experience, he gave me the gift of a life lesson. Great coaches always coach when they are around those in need. When I heard that Roy Williams was retiring, I thought to myself, "He may not coach the Tar Heels anymore, but a coach never stops coaching." Roy will never stop "coaching" when it comes to helping someone in need. The great coaches never really retire; it is in their blood to instruct, give guidance, encourage and lift the spirits of others.

The rules of golf and the Bible are similar. One was written to help a golfer who has lost his way on the course, while the scriptures provide structure and guidance for living an abundant, healthy life through the examples of Jesus Christ. But, without instruction from a teacher providing clarity and understanding, these rules for the links and life sometimes go wasted and become misunderstood, leading to penalties on and off the course. Thank you, Roy, for interpreting the rules of golf to a teenager needing guidance finding his way around the course. Your legacy will go down as a Hall of Fame coach to the rest of the world, but to me, you will always be a teacher first!

Golf Tips Magazine July/Aug 2021 Issue

As Seen Through My Eyes

by

Dr. Matt Mingione

Maternal Fetal Medicine Specialist, Columbus, Ohio

I work in a highly technical field of medicine that involves a large amount of risk. My job is pressure-packed, requiring me to always overthink all things at all times, or the results could be disastrous. Unfortunately, overthinking is not the best mental habit for the game of golf. I first met Jon while I was looking for a coach for my son, who was starting high school golf. During the first lesson, it quickly became apparent that Jon had a gift for teaching. He didn't overload Sam with technical details. Instead, he provided honest feedback with a kindness that allowed my son to be open to trying things a different way. Halfway through that first lesson, I knew that this was the kind of coaching that I also needed.

Over the next three years, Jon helped me drop my index from an 18 to a 7.7. He provided critical instruction, but more than that, he embraced my style of learning and my values, and he met me where I was to achieve success. In my eyes, Jon is more of a golf mentor than a golf coach. He truly cares that I love golf, which we all know can be one of the most frustrating games in the world. Jon's kindness is apparent, but I think it's his gentle humor that I appreciate the most.

Now, when I am struggling during a round, I often fall back on one lesson when Jon told me one of my favorite jokes, at my own expense. I was trying to master a new move, and Jon was encouraging me to speed up my routine. I said, "Jon, I need to think about this." He replied, "Matt, I would never underestimate your ability to overthink a shot." I realized his comment was honest, kind and true, and we both had a good laugh over it. In every lesson, it is so clear to me that Jon's commitment is to only put good into this world. Golf may be the conduit, but faith is the driver. I am lucky to call Jon coach and blessed to call him friend.

CHAPTER 17

PERSPECTIVE FROM THE GREEN

"Therefore, if anyone is in Christ, he is a new creation.
The old has passed away; behold, the new has come."
(2 Corinthians 5:17)

I recently had a playing lesson with one of my regular students, Dr. Matt Mingione, a maternal fetal medicine specialist from the Columbus, Ohio, area. We have been working together since the late fall of 2020, and when we started, Dr. Mingione was an 18-handicap golfer. I noticed immediately his natural power, that he is very athletic and, like most surgeons I teach, has great touch around the green. We met weekly, and from a coach's vantage point, Dr. Mingione was doing great! His swing changes on the driving range were starting to take shape, and the video proved that progress was being made; however, his scorecard revealed a much different story. I needed to see him in action to witness firsthand why my student was struggling, so I decided that our lesson time would be better spent on the golf course, not in front of a basket of balls. I knew the course would give me the perspective needed to better guide his progress.

We scheduled the playing lesson, and I told Dr. Mingione, "I want to watch you play the first hole without any guidance. Do what you normally do and pretend I am not here." The first hole didn't go well. As we stood on the second hole tee box, an intimidating par 3 over water to a tucked pin behind a bunker, I began to see anxiety set into my student's face. Now, during a typical day of work, Dr. Mingione operates on babies while the fetus is still inside the mother's womb. Often during the surgeries, the baby's small hand will push the surgeon's instrument away from its body as if to say, "Keep that thing away from me," a fact he divulged to me not too long ago and one that only magnifies the pressure that elite surgeons work under daily.

I looked at Dr. Mingione as he stood on the tee box and could tell his wheels were turning. It was as if he were mentally rehearsing every swing tip we had discussed over the last year and a half. He made a few practice swings, and then his body began to freeze up. He backed away from the ball and looked at me and said, "This is what happens to me on the course, Jon. I get over a difficult shot like this, and I get so nervous and lose focus on what I should do next." I looked at him and said without hesitation, "Doc, you perform surgeries on babies inside of a mother's womb and you are nervous over this shot? Stick to your pre-shot routine and do the best you can." He looked at me, laughed and said, "You're right, Jon. I've never thought of it that way." From that moment on, his perspective on the golf course changed, and it was a pivotal moment in his growth as a player.

One of my favorite lessons is the playing lesson. It's fun to get off the driving range and onto the golf course where I learned to play as a child. The real key to these lessons is getting a student out of his or her thoughts on swing technique and teach him or her to look at the golf course from the perspective of the architect. Architects build golf courses with one very key thought: "Where are we moving the water?" Greens are built to drain; ponds are built in low areas to handle sudden rains and keep the water from standing on the course and creating puddles. I insist that all my students pay attention to these low areas around the greens for one very important reason — the golf ball will tend to roll in that direction. I also insist that students start reading the greens as they approach the green, often from hundreds of yards away. I encourage them to feel the slopes in the greens, not with their hands but with their feet. I've always said, "Your eyes will lie to you, but your feet never will." By walking onto the green and up to the hole, a player has a much better perspective for the terrain ahead of them in route to the cup.

Another critical component to a playing lesson is understanding the correct side of the tee box to tee the ball up. Very rarely will PGA TOUR players tee the ball in the middle of the tee box. The course management rules for teeing the ball are very simple. If the trouble is on the right side, tee the ball on the right side. Teeing the ball on the right side of the tee box opens the left side of the fairway or green visually. If the trouble is on the left side of the fairway or green, tee the ball on the left side of the tee box. Teeing the ball on the left side opens the right side of the fairway or green visually. If the trouble is on both sides, a player must know his normal ball flight (fade tee up on the right and draw tee up on the left). By using both sides of the tee box, a player's perspective of the hole changes visually and improves the odds of hitting the fairway by making the fairway as wide as possible.

Another perspective that most players seldom look at is the perspective from the green looking back. The next time you play golf, stand on the green and look back toward the tee box. Notice the widest part of the fairways, look for the narrow parts and notice how the bunkers seem less intimidating because you are no longer facing the sand. The widest part is where the architect gives you the most room to land the ball. Good players seek the forgiveness of this spacious area and, if they are using good course management skills, may hit a fairway wood or hybrid to this safety zone to eliminate the perils of the sand and water.

Perspective is also important in the game of life. One day just after my divorce and a long frustrating day of teaching golf, I walked back to my car and silently said a prayer. With tears welling in my eyes, I asked God for some sort of sign that things were going to be okay. I then looked up to my right toward the west and saw the most beautiful sunset I had ever seen across the Ohio landscape. I stopped, stood in awe of God's masterpiece and savored the moment. I felt total peace. With no one else around, I walked to my car and drove home. That night, I got on social media where one of my friends from the area had posted a picture of the same sunset, but from a totally different angle. His perspective in the picture showed a sunset with buildings and power lines, while my memory was of a beautiful golf course with open fields. It suddenly hit me like a bolt of lightning and was the sign I was seeking. I realized that I was the only person in the world at that exact time, exact moment and exact place who saw that sunset from that unique perspective. Every day God gives us signs from His playground Mother Earth, and most of us take them for granted and then say to ourselves, "When was the last time God showed up in my life?" Take the time today to go on a hike or watch the sun rise or set, and you will feel God's presence. That day taught me a lot about God's perspective and how He communicates to me every day, if I take the time to listen. God not only answered my prayer, but He did it in a way that I still recall on days when life doesn't seem to be going my way.

The scriptures say that God forms us all while we are in our mother's womb. I believe that it is during this time that He adds a unique purpose to our life before we are ever born. The older I get, the more I realize that my ways and my plans for life may not be God's will. As impossible as it may seem, I try to look at my journey, fraught with some successes and all too many failures, and try to look at myself the way God sees me, as His child. I try to imagine God, the master architect, standing on the green of my life looking back at all the things I have done. Will He focus on my mistakes, like the bunkers and the penalty areas that guard the fairways and greens, or will he see spacious fairways of forgiveness and mercy? Through my Savior, Jesus Christ who died for all our sins, I am inclined to believe that, no matter how messed up my swing may have been in the past and how many bunkers, creeks, ponds and trees my ball may have found, I am forgiven. Through repentance and His grace, my ball will eventually find the short green grass of Heaven, with Jesus waiting and smiling with open arms.

Through a lot of hard work and less than two years later, Dr. Mingione has dropped from an 18 handicap down to a 7.7. He recently sent me a text that would make any coach proud. It simply read, "Jon! I just shot 74! My best score ever!" This news obviously brings me happiness as a teaching professional seeing success from a student who has put in the time and practice to improve his swing. But I know the real progress in his game was not the improvement of his golf swing over the last year and a half. The "aha moment" for him started during our time on the course, when he looked at a very difficult situation and simply changed his perspective.

Golf Tips Magazine Sept/Oct 2022 Issue

<h1 style="text-align:center">CHAPTER 18</h1>

<h2 style="text-align:center">THE BUNKER RAKE</h2>

"…You shall love your neighbor as yourself. There is no other commandment greater than these." (Mark 12:31)

Over the years, junior golf camps have made up a large part of my summer schedule. I have been teaching junior camps for almost three decades and have gotten to the point in my life where my former campers are now married and have young golfers of their own. As a man who was not blessed to be a father, teaching junior golfers fills a void in my life, even if it is only for a few hours a day. I've always said, "The good news for me is that I get to spend time with the kids, but I don't have to pay for their college education!" There is nothing like watching the reaction of children after a great shot, as their eyes widen and a smile comes rolling across their face. This simple act of expression brings joy to my heart and rekindles childhood memories from my experiences learning the game. Junior camps include full swing, putting, chipping, bunker, pitching and on-course instruction as well as rules and etiquette. I want all the camp activities to be a learning experience but also fun, so we include games and contests to add to their experience.

One of the favorite subjects for junior campers is when we cover bunker play. For most adults playing the game, the idea of going into the bunker is the same feeling as going to the dentist with a toothache. However, for kids the bunker is like a sand box, full of fun and excitement. The kids gravitate to the sandy beach like summer vacationers on Independence Day. For the instructors involved, teaching the juniors how to escape from the perils of the bunkers can get dirty by day's end. After camps, I find sand inside my shoes, in my hair and on the back of my neck, making me feel as if I have spent the day sunning at the beach. Unfortunately for me and the other instructors, there is no ocean to dive into to rinse off the day's work.

Before ever hitting a shot or starting the technical aspect of bunker instruction, I sit the kids down and have a very important talk about the etiquette of the bunker. I cover where to enter and exit the bunker and emphasize two important rules of etiquette before ever hitting a shot. Rule number one is to find the bunker rake and rule number two is to rake the bunker before you exit. I then demonstrate how to properly rake the bunker.

Locating and finding the rake before you enter the bunker speeds up play. Many golfers have little to no foresight in locating the bunker rake; they simply hit their shot and realize the rake is on the other side of the sand. I have seen players walk through the sand to pick up the rake after playing their shot and often seen players neglect to rake the bunker at all. Some players simply brush the sand around after their shot with the bottom of their golf shoes and walk out, leaving a mess for the less fortunate players coming behind. In a perfect world, the bunker should be left in a better condition when you exit the sand than when you first entered it. I emphasize this to all my students and remind them that a sure-fire way to get in trouble with the group behind you is to not rake the sand after your shot.

The bunker rake is a symbol for golf etiquette, and the act of raking the bunker is a golfer's way of paying respect to the golf course so that others can play from pristine conditions. Golf is the only sport I know where you help your opponents play their next shot. In basketball, you attempt to block a shot. In football, you tackle and defend a territory, but in golf, you clear the way for others by making the playing surface better than you found it for your opponent. Oh, how I wish our society would learn the lessons from the symbolism of the bunker rake and the other examples of etiquette from the game of golf.

During the winter months, my fiancé and I escape the cold, dreary, grey skies of Ohio to reside in Bonita Springs, Florida.

We bought the home in March of 2022. Seven months later, the area near our home, along with the entire southwest coastline of Florida, was devastated by Hurricane Ian. Our home butts up to a canal that feeds into the Imperial River, a winding, snake-like river that leads directly into the Gulf of Mexico. Although the area was decimated by the near Category 5 hurricane, our home was spared from flooding. On New Years Day 2023, we rented a boat and made our maiden voyage up and down the river. Excited to see the river for the first time, the three-hour boat trip opened my eyes to the damage in the area that was reminiscent of Armageddon.

Although our trip revealed the beauty of the river lined with mangrove trees, we spotted a strange floating buoy off in the distant water. As our boat approached the buoy, we noticed underneath it in the middle of the river lay a sunken upside-down car. Some other debris lining the shoreline was recognizable, including a basketball goal and refrigerator, while other items were simply shredded plastic that draped the mangrove and cypress trees like confetti on New Year's Eve. Drifting wood from decimated docks littered the waterway and was like floating mines. Household trash was everywhere. I could not believe the devastation and wondered how in the world this normally beautiful ecosystem would ever get cleaned up. I must admit, when we returned our rental boat, my memories were not of the dolphins and wildlife we saw but of the debris and trash that littered the waterway.

Every morning, I love to sit on the lanai of our home and look out at the waterway lined with boats. I love to see whether the tide is coming in or going out. Since Hurricane Ian, I started noticing floating debris in our canal. I looked at the trash and could feel the Holy Spirit speak to my mind and heart. I suddenly saw a vision in the recesses of my mind; the vision was of a bunker rake. I didn't understand the vision at first but then heard a question in my mind, "If not you, then who?" At that moment, I knew that I was supposed to clean up the floating plastic cooler top, bottles and trash in the canal that had been delivered by the morning tide. I then asked myself, "If I don't do it, then who will?" Cleaning the floating debris that morning was the start of something new and became a part of my daily routine. Each morning, I would start my day by grabbing the pool skimmer and walking down to the canal to fish out my catch for the day.

I am convinced that one of the reasons I felt compelled to clean out the canal daily was because of the many lessons I learned from the game of golf. Golf teaches so many life lessons, many that have nothing to do with the score you write down on the card. I also believe that the Holy Spirit had a big influence as well as my upbringing from my parents, who taught me that our surrounding environment is a gift from God that must be respected. These lessons from life and golf are magnified even more as an adult, as I began delving into the Bible on a regular basis.

In Mark 12, one of the scribes comes to Jesus and asks Him, *"Which is the first commandment of all?" Jesus answered, … "And you shall love the Lord your God with all your heart, with all your soul, with all your mind, and with all your strength. This is the first commandment. And the second, like it, is this: 'You shall love your neighbor as yourself.' There is no other commandment greater than these." (Mark 12:29-31).* When I recently read that scripture, one word stood out to me, not because of its religious importance but because of its vagueness. That word was "neighbor."

Is the neighbor the house beside mine or my neighborhood? Is the neighbor the community of Bonita Springs or the state of Florida? Is the neighbor the United States or the entire world? I believe you can make a case that the answer is all the above. Based on the lessons learned from golf and the bunker rake, I would make the argument that the neighbor to which Jesus was referring was even more vast than people; the neighbor also includes our environment and the fish and animals that inhabit it. Like searching for the bunker rake after our ball has rolled off the fairway and into the sand, taking care of the environment and picking up the trash in the areas we live in brings beauty and harmony to the world God gave us that we all must share.

By raking the bunker, a golfer selflessly takes extra time to improve the damage from the shot last played, but also sets the table for the next person whose ball has found a similar fate. This act of thoughtfulness is a small example of what Jesus was saying about "loving thy neighbor." Whether picking up trash that others have left behind, helping elderly neighbors with their yard work or donating time at a food bank, these small acts of kindness may go unnoticed by others, but they are never unnoticed by God. So, the next time your ball finds the bunker, seek the bunker rake first, play the shot to the best of your ability and pay it forward by leaving the sand a better place for those to come.

Golf Tips Magazine July/Aug 2023 Issue

Chapter 19

The Mountain

"...but also if you say to this mountain, 'Be removed and be cast into the sea,' it will be done. And whatever things you ask for in prayer, believing, you will receive." (Matthew 21:21-22)

One of the biggest mistakes I see many golf teachers make during lessons is simple—they spend too much time focusing on the problem. In a typical one-hour lesson, I spend no more than 15 minutes showing students their swing issues on video or giving them launch monitor data. I then use the technology at the end of the lesson to show the improvement. Why? I try not to focus on the problem—I focus on the solution!

I try my best to incorporate this mentality into my life as well; however, sometimes my problems are so big and so high that they appear to be a mountain standing before me. As a teenager, newly exposed to tournament golf, I noticed that during the tournaments, the lake seemed larger, the trees were suddenly taller, and the short tap-in putts I never missed seemed longer. I had created a mountain for only my mind to see.

Instead of focusing on where I wanted my golf ball to go, I focused on the negative — the mountain that stood before me. This mountain mentality also translates to life. What are your mountains? Cancer diagnosis? Debt? Divorce? Drug abuse? The list of life's mountains is too long, too high for any one person to handle, let alone comprehend.

Jesus described life's problems as "mountains" to His disciples. Mountains appear in everyone's lives. The key is not the mountain but our focus.

I believe that God allows mountains to come into our lives for a simple reason. Are we going to focus on God or the mountain? The mountain may be gigantic, but God is bigger. Remember, God knew about the mountain well before you did. Go to God first, speak to the mountain, and then cast it into the vast sea of His love. Believe in God first! Then put your faith in doctors, counselors, family and friends. Believe and then receive His mercy and grace. Instead of looking up to the mountain, you will be standing on its peak and enjoying the view!

Golf Tips Magazine July/Aug 2020 Issue

CHAPTER 20

A Positive Mindset:

One Shot and Day at a Time…

"See what kind of love the Father has given to us, that we should be called children of God; and so we are. The reason why the world does not know us is that it did not know him."
(1 John 3:1)

I am a firm believer in the following quote: "You will ultimately become in life what you think of yourself." Understanding this quote is essential to a healthy lifestyle and crucial to the mindset of a successful golfer. Years ago, while working at the Grand Cypress Academy of Golf, one of my co-workers shared a conversation he had with former PGA TOUR player Brad Faxon. Brad said to him, "Just because you make a double bogey, that doesn't mean you are a bad person." Looking back at that remark, I now understand the wisdom behind those words. Golfers often relate their self-worth to the scores they have per hole, and quite often, their attitude on the course starts to mirror their errant drives or missed putts. Golf is supposed to be a leisure activity, but by the time the round is over, most golfers' thoughts are drowned in the 19th hole and recounted to anyone who will listen. As the old saying goes, "misery loves company."

The best players in the world have the unique ability to play one shot at a time. Bad shot, go to the next shot; great shot, go to the next shot, without allowing the last shot, either good or bad, to affect what lies ahead. But, even the best players in the world can struggle with this concept. Here is a tip: After each shot, allow yourself 15 seconds to let go, regardless of the shot, then move on. Fifteen seconds of venting or celebrating is OK, as long as the focus returns to the next shot. This practice is much easier said than done.

In the game of life, where your score really matters, your success can be determined by your self-belief. Take a moment each day to try this simple exercise. Stand in front of a mirror, look into your eyes and say, "I am a child of God and I am loved." Never forget these words, because God loves you more than you love yourself. This simple exercise chips away at what the world may say. More importantly, hearing yourself say the words, "I am a child of God," reminds you not of who you are but of "whose" you are. This positive mindset is the key to mental health as well as self-esteem, and from your lips, your own words remind your own ears that God is in control of your life and that He is the Father and you are the child.

It is comforting to know that we have a Creator who loves us, and in the game of life, He can turn our double bogey into a birdie, one day at a time…

Golf Tips Magazine Sept/Oct 2020 Issue

CHAPTER 21

IN GOD WE TRUST

"And immediately Jesus stretched out His hand and caught him, and said to him, 'O you of little faith, why did you doubt?" (Matthew 14: 31-32)

Trust is a word that is often associated with the game of golf. "I didn't trust my swing" or "I didn't trust the read of the putt" are two of the more common responses I hear from players who underperformed under the pressure of tournament golf. I often hear these comments, not from high handicappers but from top-level players I have worked with over my career, including PGA and LPGA players. I have always said, "My problems in golf start here (I then point to the right side of my head) and end here," as I point to the left side. Bobby Jones summed it up best: "Golf is a game that is played on a five-inch course — the distance between your ears."

My road to becoming a PGA of America member started in Florida in 1992 by picking the driving range at the Grand Cypress Academy of Golf. One of my co-workers was Jay Williamson. After several years of picking range balls, Jay worked his way off the driving range and mini tours of Florida onto the biggest stage in golf, the PGA TOUR. He earned his card in 1994 and had a wonderful 16-year career. I recall asking Jay one afternoon about his life on the tour as a rookie. He replied, "When you arrive at the event on Monday, the pressure slowly builds. It's like putting your head into a vice, and at the end of each day, the vice gets twisted another notch tighter." Jay's comments illustrate the harsh realities of life on the PGA TOUR. It is not as glamorous as it appears on television.

To be a PGA TOUR player, you must be willing to put your life, career and game on the line. Professional golf, for the most part, is an individual sport played against an entire field, not a single opponent, and, oh, by the way, the field never plays poorly. If you hit a poor shot or have a bad day on the links, there is really no one to blame but yourself as you watch the players from the field who fared better that day rise up the leaderboard. Tournament golf at the highest level requires first and foremost that a player trust each shot, as well as trust in the decision-making process between player and caddie. This trust is needed each week to maneuver through the four-day, 72-hole marathon of the PGA TOUR. The game is unlike any other sport I have played, and without trust in all the decisions that take place during a single round of golf, the battle is often lost before the tee ever goes to the ground.

Over my career, I have experienced tournament pressure, but nothing like what Jay experienced. However, in 2008 my career would be forever changed as I got a taste of what Jay experienced, not as a PGA TOUR player but as a PGA TOUR coach. In May of that year, I started working with Bob Sowards as his swing coach the week of the Memorial Tournament in Columbus, Ohio. I had taught aspiring mini tour players, coached at the 2007 Women's U.S. Open the year before and worked with some LPGA players in my career, but had never obtained full-time status as a coach on the biggest stage in golf. I would be lying if I said that I wasn't nervous or didn't feel pressure. Ideally, I needed to be working with Bob for a minimum of six months before his first event in January in Hawaii, not the week before his tournament at Muirfield Village. The first two weeks as Bob's coach resulted in missed cuts, and then Bob took a week off to return home. Finally, we found some time for us to work on his swing. Over the summer, Bob's game continued to improve, and by the end of August, he finished ninth at the Wyndham Championship in Greensboro, North Carolina. He continued his hot play into the fall season, including a final nine hole 29 at the Texas Open.

During the summer of 2008, I experienced a baptism by fire, working as a full-time director of instruction at the New Albany Country Club as well as a full-time PGA TOUR coach. During that time, I realized the biggest struggle elite players face in golf is not their swing changes, but trusting changes made in their setup. In Bob's case, we moved the golf ball more forward in his stance. Bob played the ball too far back, resulting in a knee drive toward the target and deep pivots. By August of 2008, Bob trusted his setup and was rotating beautifully, creating shallow divots and clipping the ball off the tight fairways of the tour. Over the summer, Bob began to fully trust the setup changes we had made as player and coach. He originally did not want me to change his short game, but over time, he trusted me enough to change his approach to chipping, bunker play, pitching and putting. During this process, trust must be earned between the instructor and the student. The same can be said about life as well.

Trust must be earned in life, especially in relationships. I would never give my Social Security number to a stranger, but I would share that personal information with my parents. Why? Because they have earned my trust, they have always been there for me, and I know if I ever needed them during an emergency, they would drop everything to help. I'm sure my siblings would say the same. My parents spent a lifetime reinforcing the trust between two parents and their children by always showing up. This act of love cemented that bond of trust and is something I try to never take for granted. Looking back over my life, I can think of countless examples of my parents' love for me and my siblings; however, there is one story that stands out, and its message is still etched in my mind until this very day.

As a young, blond-haired boy, I remember playing in the front yard of our home on Airport Road in Bryson City, North Carolina. Our small brick home was built on top of a steep hill. The front of the home was a one-story while the back was a two-story with a walk-out basement. As I was playing in the front yard, I noticed my father walking along the top of our roof. I watched from the ground in amazement as my father bravely navigated the sloped roof, working his way toward the chimney to fix the television antenna, located at the roof's peak. I looked at the ladder leaning against the house and yelled up to my father, "Dad can I come up on the roof with you?" My father looked down from above and replied, "Yes. Be sure to look upward as you step up the ladder." As a 7-year-old, this was about the coolest thing I had ever attempted. As I carefully placed my foot on the first rung of the ladder and stepped toward the second rung, I made sure to look up, like my father had suggested. I noticed my surroundings began to change. With each step, I saw nothing but bricks and soffit in front of me, but as I reached the top, I saw a sea of brown shingles and a beautiful blue sky. I immediately felt the security of my father's strong hand as he grabbed me by the arm. It took me a few seconds to get my bearings and adjust to the pitched slope of the roof. Each step was a new adventure, and I can still hear the shingles as they crackled beneath my feet. I felt as though I could touch the sky and was utterly amazed at the new perspective of my neighborhood and its surroundings. I looked for my friends to let them know of my daring adventure but found no one outside to yell the good news. I felt a sense of pride as I stood beside my father and honestly never felt safer. I knew my father was there for me, and at that moment, that was all I needed.

My father's work on the roof now complete, he looked at me and said, "Jon, I am going down the ladder first. Once I get to the bottom, you can come down." As my father began stepping down the ladder, I started noticing how high we were off the ground. I also noticed that first step of the ladder and wondered if I could get my foot on it without knocking the ladder over or, worse yet, falling. At that moment, fear struck me, and I began to feel isolated and alone. Even though I could see my father, I felt the separation.

My father, now safely on the ground, suddenly did the unthinkable. He picked up the ladder leaning against the house and laid it onto the ground. I was in shock! Dad then looked at me and said, "Jon, I want you to jump to me, and I will catch you." I couldn't believe it! Tears began to well up in my blue eyes and I said, "No dad, I can't do that. I'm scared!" "Jon, I want you to trust me," my father replied calmly. This conversation between father and son went on for minutes as I nervously stood on the edge of the roof. My mind began to wonder in fear, "What if he misses me, or what if I am too heavy and he drops me?" Warm tears began rolling down my face as my father stood there calmly, feet firmly on the ground with open arms. He once again said to me, "Trust me Jon. I will catch you."

I knew at that moment I had no choice, so I opened my arms, trusted my father would catch me and took a leap of faith. I safely fell into my father's strong arms; it was a moment I will never forget. Dad held me in his arms tightly, kissed me on my right cheek and said, "Jon, I love you and I would never let anything happen to you. I wanted you to trust me." As he let me down from his arms, my feet hit the ground safely. At that moment, a bond was cemented between father and son as I hurried off to tell my mother. Let's just say she wasn't as thrilled with my father at that moment and his approach to teaching their eldest child about trust.

When I think back to this story, I am reminded of the story from the Bible of Jesus walking on the water. In Matthew 14, Peter and the disciples were traveling by boat to the other side of the Sea of Galilee when the boat came upon a storm. The disciples saw Jesus in the distance, walking toward them on the water. Peter yelled out to Jesus and asked if he could walk with Him. Jesus replied, "Come." Peter confidently got out of the boat and started walking toward Jesus. As Peter left the vicinity of the boat and got out into the open water, the storm worsened, the waves grew higher and Peter became scared. Peter began to sink beneath the water as the disciples watched in disbelief. At that moment, Jesus, still firmly standing on the water, reached into the sea, grabbed Peter by the hand and pulled him safely into the boat.

When my father was standing in front of me on the ground below, I felt like Peter, alone and scared while separated from my father. But my father caught me safely and was true to his word.

Jesus, a man who had performed countless miracles witnessed by the disciples, was now miraculously walking on water. He was standing in front of Peter and the disciples, and yet Peter did not trust him because he was distracted by the wind and the waves of the storm that surrounded the boat. Peter's lack of faith demonstrated how humans tend to trust in only what we can see, understand and define. However, God's infinite power cannot be defined by man; if so, He would not be worth worshipping. Trusting God requires faith, believing in the unknown, believing in miracles and understanding that He is always standing with us with open arms. All He asks is that we trust.

In the game of golf, I can trust myself, I can trust my swing, and I can trust in my coach, but in the end, all of them, in some way, over time, will let me down. On the PGA TOUR, there is a razor-sharp fine line between winning and missing the cut. In most cases, the problems are not in the physical realm of the swing but in the mental psyche of the player. I spent 12 years as Bob's swing coach, and over that time we not only created a bond of trust between player and coach, but we also became good friends. I still consider that time spent together as one of the highlights of my career, but like all things in life, change happens.

Relationships are always growing. They are either growing closer or they are growing apart. Trust can be earned between parent and child, between brother and sister or between the closest of friends, but in the end, all these relationships, at times, will let you down. Ultimately, true trust can only come from one source, and that one source is God. Trust in God requires that we believe in Him and trust His plan for our life. It also requires that, when we ask Him to lead us, we listen to Him and then follow His lead. This fact was illustrated to me one April morning, almost two years after my first book was published.

I will never forget that morning as I bowed my head in prayer and asked God, "What is next for my life?" I closed my eyes after the question and saw a vision in my mind. Like the opening scene of a movie, I saw the letter "T" slowly roll across the screen in my mind from right to left. It was immediately followed by the letter

"R," then "U," then "S" and finally "T." In front of me, I saw the word "trust." I then saw a vision of myself playing in my front yard in Bryson City, yelling up to my father and then stepping up the ladder to his waiting arms. I saw myself walking confidently with him on the roof, standing on the edge of the roofline, crying in fear and finally trusting him as I jumped into his arms. I could feel my father holding me like it was yesterday and felt his razor-stubbled face kiss me on my cheek. The vision now over, I opened my eyes and thought, "Why did God show me this memory? What does this mean?" As I sat in solitude in my leather recliner, contemplating what had just transpired, I decided to continue my morning routine. I reached for my David Jeremiah devotional book, *Quest: Seeking God Daily*, and began reading the devotional for April 8th. I read the following:

"A young boy was out in the country, climbing among a row of cliffs. He yelled from the top of one, 'Hey dad! Catch me!' The father turned around to see his son joyfully jumping off a rock straight at him. The dad became an instant circus act, catching his son, causing them both to fall to the ground. When the father found his voice, he gasped in exasperation, 'Son, can you give me one good reason why you did that?' He responded with remarkable calmness: 'Sure... because you're my dad.' His whole assurance was based on the fact that his father was trustworthy.'"

I was in complete shock! I couldn't believe the sequence of events that had just unfolded. After reading those words, I knew that God was asking me to write another book. I had no idea of the book's title but knew that the story of me jumping into my father's waiting arms would somehow be used in it. Looking back, I wish I had trusted my earthly father, like the boy from the devotional trusted his. Now, my Heavenly Father had laid the foundation for the next journey in my life – a second book. I had learned my lessons from the past and refused to allow the storms of uncertainty to hinder my decision. I responded, "Yes, Father, I trust you."

God was asking me to take another leap of faith and to stretch myself as a novice writer. I didn't yet know the details or the plan for the book, but I was confident in one thing: God knew. God certainly has a plan for all His children. Like Peter asking Jesus if he can walk on water during the storm to be by His side, sometimes you must look at the impossible circumstances of your life and know that, through Christ, all things are possible. God's arms are wide open, and He is waiting for you to take the leap of faith, to fall safely into His strong arms and to put your trust in Him.

Golf Tips Magazine Sept/Oct 2023 Issue

CHAPTER 22

THE MODEL SWING

"Thomas said to Him, 'Lord, we do not know where You are going, and how can we know the way?' Jesus said to him, 'I am the way, the truth and the life. No one comes to the Father except through Me.'" (John 14: 5-6)

In December of 1992, I met Dr. Ralph Mann while working at the Grand Cypress Academy of Golf. I do not remember our introduction, but I do remember the first time I saw his model overlay system. Dr. Mann is a scientist and former Olympic athlete, and he has a doctoral degree in biomechanics. Through Dr. Mann's research, I now have a better understanding of how the human body works, how elite golfers produce power during the golf swing and the strategies tour players use in the short game. During my 20-year span at Grand Cypress, I was privileged to teach with his model overlay system called SwingModel (formerly ModelGolf). The two-decade span at Grand Cypress left a lasting impression in my mind – a blueprint that I now clearly see with every student I teach.

Dr. Mann was a silver medalist in the 400-meter-high hurdles in the 1972 Olympics held in Munich, Germany. Unfortunately, those Olympic games were marred by the kidnapping and killing of 11 Israeli athletes and coaches and a West German police officer by Palestinian Black September members. Dr. Mann was not competing that day and was hiking in the Austrian Alps with his wife, Jackie. When they returned to the Olympic Village, they saw tanks roaming the streets and knew something was terribly wrong.

During Dr. Mann's silver medal performance, he broke the world record for the 400-meter hurdles with a time of 48.51 seconds but unfortunately lost to John Akii-Bua of Uganda, who set a new world record time that day of 47.82 seconds. Dr. Mann often said that the reason he achieved success reaching medal status had less to do with talent and more to do with the refinement of his hurdling technique.

Dr. Mann competing in the 1972 Olympics. Photo courtesy of Dr. Ralph Mann.

Dr. Mann's first love was track and field, not golf. After the Olympics, his interest grew in helping other athletes develop and refine their track and field technique. Dr. Mann was also fascinated by how the human body performed, so he pursued his passion for sports movements at Washington State University, where he completed his doctorate in biomechanics. His dream now was to help other track and field athletes chase their dreams of Olympic gold.

Dr. Mann was instrumental in developing a model that was based on research into elite athletes' performances. For example, he studied elite sprinters and compared them to how the average sprinters performed. This first started by filming with high-speed video cameras both the elite sprinters and the average sprinters while they ran. The computer software system, developed by Dr. Mann, would then compare the tendencies of the elite versus the average sprinters. The computer would exclude the common tendencies of the elite and average sprinters, or, simply put, the computer would throw out what they both had in common. The computer would then highlight what the elite sprinters were doing that was different from the average sprinters.

Dr. Mann using the model overlay system to teach athletes to refine their technique. Photo courtesy Dr. Ralph Mann.

The computer software system had the ability to look at thousands of different movements of the human body. The software system would plot specific points of the body (for example, the knee) and then use statistics to measure the movements. His research was about using statistics to highlight these differences to find the truth. Through Dr. Mann's research, science was used to show a track and field coach and his student how the elite athletes best performed. His research often disproved old ways of teaching that were often based on opinion. To Dr. Mann, the numbers were the truth, and the numbers didn't lie.

During the early 1980s, Chuck Cooke, the director of the Hills of Lakeway Academy of Golf in Austin, Texas, was intrigued about the research being done by Dr. Mann and invited him to bring his software technology to Austin. The first elite player Dr. Mann filmed with high-speed-video was Tom Kite. While spending time in Austin, Dr. Mann met Fred Griffin and Phil Rodgers. Rodgers was instrumental in getting other tour players to come and be filmed by Dr. Mann, including Jack Nicklaus and

Greg Norman. In the end, Dr. Mann filmed 54 tour players and then filmed club professionals to quantify the differences. The computer software threw out the similarities of what the PGA TOUR player and club professional both had in common and focused on what they did differently in their golf swings. Over time, this research gave birth to the first "swing model."

The model now complete, Dr. Mann filmed the Hills of Lakeway Academy school students, built the model to the student's body size, and then superimposed the model's skeletal figure over the student's setup. Dr. Mann then looked at the student's swing and the model's swing, frame by frame, over 10 positions. The positions started with the setup and finished with the follow-through. This groundbreaking technology made it easy for both the student and the teacher to see the differences between the student's golf swing and the model's swing. Griffin and Rodgers loved the technology so much that when Jack Nicklaus built his first academy at Grand Cypress, they asked Dr. Mann to move his CompuSport company's headquarters to Orlando. This move in 1985 gave birth to one of the first golf schools in the world that was rooted in state-of-the-art science, a never-before-seen model overlay software system for golf and an amazing teaching staff.

My time at Grand Cypress introduced technology and information to me that I had never seen or heard of before, and God planted me into a cocoon where I was privileged to learn from some of the greatest teachers in the world. This developmental phase of my career formed who I am today as a teacher by exposing me to the science of the golf swing. Over time, I learned to communicate this technical knowledge to my eager students, doing so in a way that they could understand. I learned very quickly that one of the greatest gifts a teacher can possess is the ability to take something that is very complex and present it in a way that is very easy to understand.

In my own life, I struggled with science until I met Dr. Mann. I was a "feel player" when I initially arrived at Grand Cypress. I was fascinated with his model overlay system but had difficulty implementing it into my own golf swing. It took years of hard work and practice to break the old, outdated habits in my swing and follow a new approach. I knew this new approach, in the long run, would make me a better player. The years teaching with the model helped me as both a player and as a teacher.

When thinking about my time learning the science of the golf swing, I think about my daily time with the Lord. I often struggle to understand the "science" of the Bible and have come to terms with the fact that at some point, faith must step into the equation. The Bible is recorded history from thousands of years ago. Records were kept on scrolls in those days, and eyewitness accounts were the high-speed-video of the time. I will be the first to admit that I struggle with the technical writings of Paul in Romans. I tend to gravitate to the many parables from Jesus in the Gospels. I love the Psalms and am especially drawn to the Gospel of John. I will spend my entire life studying the golf swing and the Bible, but I will never, ever fully understand all that they both have to offer. Through teaching golf and as a Christian author, my goal is simple – to make the complexities of both easier to understand.

When it comes to Christianity, I am not an expert. I have never been trained in religion. My science comes through years of experience going to church, reading the Bible, living life, daily prayer and trying my best to help others. I try to listen to God when I write through the Holy Spirit. I often hear the world telling me to trust and believe the science of the world and to not put my faith in God. But I have chosen to listen less to the world, social media and the mainstream media and listen more to my Heavenly Father and the Word of God. Over my lifetime, I have come to the conclusion that science is simply man's attempt at trying to define God. But, as Dr. David Jeremiah said in his study Bible that I so often read, *"If God could be defined, He wouldn't be worth worshipping."*

The study of the world's elite sprinters focuses on what man can control – the technique. The model can't create the God-given ability of speed that elite sprinters are born with; it can only refine the technique to make it better. The model can't give average golfers the God-given abilities of Tiger Woods or the discipline of Tom Kite; it can only improve their technique. The science is defined by the quantitative numbers accumulated by years of research to help improve the performance, but the natural talents needed to excel in any sport can only be created by God. Science can help, teachers can improve, fitness and nutrition are important, but only God can create the mind, body and talent needed to perform at the highest level – or any level, for that matter.

Science and faith seek the same thing; they both seek the truth. In my life, Jesus Christ is the truth. He is my moral compass. He is my model. The examples set by His 33-year life are documented in the Bible by His disciples in the Gospels and are the examples I try to follow. Although His life was brief on Earth, His life shaped world history. More than 2,000 years later, His followers top out at more than 1 billion and are growing. Imagine having 1 billion followers on social media! If He were not the truth, His message and following would have died while He hung on the cross.

One day, I will stand before God, and He will judge the shots of my life. Some shots were well-played, while others totally missed the mark. Just as the model was created by Dr. Mann to compare golfers to the elite performers, God's standard will highlight the differences of how I chose to live my life compared to how I could have lived it. No human being can live up to God's standard, and no human being can work or earn their way into Heaven. Something we all have in common as human beings is a sinful nature. That is why the world needs a Savior!

Imagine standing before God as He takes away the sins from your life. By putting your faith in the Lord, the model Jesus Christ is superimposed over your soul for a perfect fit. Just as the computer software system removed the commonalities of the athletes to create the model, the sins from your life that are common to all human beings are removed. Now forgiven, your soul is transformed to God's standard of perfection – the way God intended you to be. Through God's grace and through our Savior's sacrifice on the cross, you live an everlasting life, free of sorrow or pain. I have chosen to put my faith in Jesus Christ as my Lord and Savior. And like I have always said to those who choose otherwise, "Today, we are all one day closer in our lifetime to finding out the truth."

Golf Tips Magazine Jan/Feb 2024 issue

CHAPTER 23

THE SLOW ROLL

"But Martha was distracted with much serving, and she approached Him and said, 'Lord, do You not care that my sister has left me to serve alone? Therefore, tell her to help me.' And Jesus answered and said to her, 'Martha, Martha, you are worried and troubled about many things. But one thing is needed, and Mary has chosen that good part, which will not be taken away from her.'" (Luke 10:40-42)

During my days of teaching the short game at the Grand Cypress Academy of Golf with Phil Rodgers, I learned the importance of using the loft of the club to dictate how far the ball rolls. Simply put, the full swing is learning how to maximize the distance of each club and the short game is learning how to control the distance of each club. The development of touch in the short game does require improved technique, but more importantly, it requires countless hours of practice. The next time you go to the driving range, look at all the golfers hitting full shots and then look toward the practice green. My bet is that, on the average day, more people will be hitting full shots with the driver than short chips from off the edge of the green.

As my mentor, Phil taught me that the best short-game players in the world use the height of the shot to stop the ball, not the spin. The height of the shot is controlled by many factors, the first being club selection. Phil's mentor was Paul Runyan, a man who won two PGA Championships and is a member of the World Golf Hall of Fame. Runyan was known not for how far he could hit the golf ball but for his ability to control how far his ball would roll in the short game. Runyan taught Rodgers a chipping method based on five clubs, the 6-iron through the pitching wedge. He would have Phil hit these shots blindfolded to develop his touch. I learned this chipping method from Phil while teaching at Grand Cypress in 1993 and have used it ever since.

Phil considered the chip shot to be an offensive shot. In other words, when he was playing on the PGA TOUR and was off the green a few yards, he was trying to make it! The shot Phil learned from Runyan and eventually taught to Jack Nicklaus was essentially a putting stroke with a lofted club. The ball would land on a spot (normally one yard onto the green) and roll to the hole. This system that Runyan taught him was known as the air-to-ground ratio. The ratios were the following:

<u>Air Time to Ground Time</u>

1 to 6	6-iron
1 to 5	7-iron
1 to 4	8-iron
1 to 3	9-iron
1 to 2	Pitching wedge

For example, if the ball is 2 yards from the edge of the green, Phil would not putt the ball through the fringe. This technique is too unpredictable, even under tour conditions. The most manicured part of the golf course is the green, so landing the ball on the green versus running it through the fringe was more predictable. Phil would then pick a spot one yard on the green (the landing spot), giving him an air time of 3 yards (ball is 2 yards off the green plus the landing area 1 yard on the green). He would then calculate the roll time (the distance from the landing spot to the hole). Let's say the distance is 15 yards. This would be a 1-to-5 ratio (3 yards of air time and 15 yards of roll time). Looking at the chart you can see that would be a 7-iron.

Phil would then take the 7-iron, set his weight forward, take his putting stroke and essentially putt with the 7-iron. The natural loft of the 7-iron would produce a lower trajectory shot that carried the ball to his spot, and then the ball would roll to the hole. This technique took away the variable (the fringe), allowing for more consistent distance control than would be produced with a putter rolling through the fringe. During his prime, Phil was more comfortable chipping from 20 to 40 feet or more from the hole than putting from the same distance from the green. The reason was that because the chipping swing was constant, it never varied; the only variable was the choice of club. In putting, the length of the swing changes on every putt, making putting the most difficult skill in golf to master.

Phil was a big believer in the club's loft doing the work, and to do this, the club needed to have a natural acceleration. The natural acceleration occurs when the player allows the gravity of the club's downswing and some rotation (mainly on higher shots) to produce the power, not the force of the arms and hands. Club selection is critical in the short game, whether going over a bunker (pitching) or hitting the lower shots (chipping). Once the player allows the club to swing, like a child swinging on a swing set, the loft of the club chosen produces the natural trajectory of the shot, allowing the ball to land softly onto the green and slowly roll to the hole. As Phil would so often say, "I like to walk the ball to the hole, baby! I like a slow roll."

The "slow roll" is a great way to think about our walk with the Lord. Before rededicating my life to Jesus Christ, I would often find myself waking up in the early morning hours after a sleep that was less than ideal. My body moved sluggishly as my mind started racing into the day ahead. I would then choose to start planning out the day's events or begin rehashing the mistakes of yesterday, and I would start to feel a knot in the pit of my stomach. I would rush to get ready for the day ahead, gobble down some breakfast, and hurry off to work. During my drive, it always seemed as though I had left something behind, as I usually arrived just minutes before my first lesson. This daily routine was certainly not what Phil had described as the "slow roll."

To produce a slower roll in my life, I now choose to lean on the Lord by starting my day reading scripture, meditating and praying. Like the chipping method taught by Runyan to Rodgers to Nickalus, I now have a system. Like Phil assessing the air-to-roll time and then choosing the proper club, I choose to wake up early to start my day first with the Lord and then assess the day ahead. This is the new daily ratio I try to live by: the time I spend focusing on Jesus versus the time I spend focusing on the world.

In golf, a player learns to trust the loft of the club to carry the ball to the landing area; the same trust is required in the Lord to carry me safely through each moment of the day. In golf, there is a natural acceleration of the club with gravity and rotation. By placing my trust in the Lord, my day naturally accelerates and my production increases. And finally, by starting my day with the Lord and choosing to follow His lead, my day seems to fall into place naturally, without the feelings of unnecessary force. When I get off track during the day, and I often do, I reconnect with short prayers while at work or out on the course to get my life back on track. This system has reduced stress and anxiety in my life and allowed me to make the most of each day.

In the short time Jesus spent with Martha and Mary, Martha was in the presence of God, and yet she chose to focus on the work of the world. On the other hand, her sister Mary chose in that moment to center and spend her time with Jesus. The Lord is always with us, even on our worst days, but we must choose to be with Him. Like the chipping system Runyan taught Rodgers that produces a slow roll to the hole, starting your day with the Lord is a system proven to never let you down. It is comforting to know that, in this fast-paced world, we can have a slow roll through the day.

Golf Tips Magazine March/April 2024 Issue

CHAPTER 24

THE COACHING TREE

Top row left to right: Todd Meena, Gus Holbrook, Fred Griffin, Adrian Stills, John Page/Bottom row left to right: Harry Zimmerman, Jon Decker, Eric Eshleman, Carl Alexander and John Pinel.

"I am the vine, you are the branches; He who abides in Me, and I in him, bears much fruit, for without Me you can do nothing." (John 15:5)

When I look back at the Grand Cypress coaching tree, I am reminded of how Jesus described "the True Vine." In this famous parable, Jesus is the vine, and God is the vinedresser or the gardener. The vine is the source of life. Some branches are barren, while others bear fruit. The vinedresser prunes the barren branches and then picks the fruit. Through the constant pruning of the barren branches and picking of the fruit, the vine remains strong, bearing fruit for generations to come.

When I think back to my time at the Grand Cypress Academy of Golf, in my mind I see a coaching tree rooted in firm soil. I see a system for teaching golf with unique individuals, who are each gifted in their ability to communicate a consistent message. I also see three men: Phil Rodgers, Fred Griffin and Dr. Ralph Mann.

Rodgers, Griffin and Mann were both the trunk of the Grand Cypress coaching tree and the vinedresser. All three men brought a different – yet important – skillset to the table, and all three pushed their young proteges by pruning and challenging us to become better, even when we thought we were already "good enough." By challenging us to improve, embrace technology and not be afraid to challenge and change our students, our team became a well-oiled machine. To Phil, Fred and Ralph, I say "thank you" for leading such an amazing coaching team and unselfishly sharing your knowledge of the game to make all of us better at our teaching craft.

The instructors were the branches of the Grand Cypress coaching tree. The knowledge that we obtained from the vine and the refinement from the pruning of the barren branches by the vinedresser shaped us over time into the instructors we are today. Because of the system of teaching that we were blessed to learn over decades at Grand Cypress, we now bear the fruits of our labor to our willing students and PGA apprentices.

In working on this writing project, I have had the opportunity to reunite with the instructors with whom I shared so much time over a cherished span of my life. I spent two decades of my life at Grand Cypress, working alongside some of the greatest teaching minds in the game today. Each of them has gone on to plant their own tree and become a vine and vinedresser at their host facility. They now willingly pass on their wisdom to young, eager apprentices, yearning to learn the game and how to better teach it. My former colleagues are now sought out for their knowledge and wisdom from the lessons learned so many years ago. Their fruit is now ripe and ready to be picked by students waiting in line for their teaching and mentoring services.

I recently reached out to all my former colleagues and asked them to share a memory of their time with Phil for this book. When I first read each of their memories of their mentor, I smiled, laughed and became emotional thinking back to my time at Grand Cypress. I hope you enjoy their personal memories. As you read them, know that this tribute could never be large enough to bear all the fruit, impact and influence that Phil's life had on the game of golf...

A Tribute to Phil Rodgers

April 3, 1938-June 26, 2018

Photo courtesy Carl Alexander

My Memories of Phil...

"HELPING OTHERS"

by

Fred Griffin

Former Director of Instruction

Grand Cypress Academy of Golf (1985-2019)

"And the things that you have heard from me among many witnesses, commit these to faithful men who will be able to teach others also." (2 Timothy 2:2)

My introduction to Phil Rodgers was in the spring of 1981. I was working as the senior instructor at The Hills of Lakeway Academy of Golf in Austin, Texas, under the direction of *Golf Magazine* Hall of Fame teacher Chuck Cook. Phil's professional playing career had ended, and his recent success helping Jack Nicklaus with his short game garnered him a lot of attention. Because the facilities at The Hills were Jack Nicklaus designed, this partnered well with Phil conducting his golf schools at this location.

Chuck arranged for Phil to visit the academy for a couple of days in advance of his golf school, along with me and the late Davis Love Jr., for an introduction to his teaching methodology.

Phil explained his chipping method that included a unique set-up, grip and ground-to-air ratio for choosing the proper club. One of our students labeled it as "the deformed wrist Hunch Back of Notre Dame chipping set-up." Next up was the patented Phil Rodgers flop shot. He first took some time to explain why he liked a certain design of the sand wedge and how important it was to have enough bounce. He likes 12 to 14 degrees of bounce for his wedges. Phil put a few balls in the rough and told Chuck and Davis to try to hit 3 to 4 inches behind the ball. He didn't like hitting down on the ball and having the hands leading the clubhead through impact. They both struggled with this concept. He would say firm and loudly, "No, no – that's not it, release the club and hit more behind the ball. Let the bounce be your friend!" Of course, Phil would take the club and drop a ball ankle deep in the rough, then take a big swing hitting the ground several inches behind the ball and landing it softly on the green close to the hole.

Phil and Chuck were instrumental in expanding the golf academy concept to other Jack Nicklaus golf course locations. It is one of the primary reasons that I became the director of the first Jack Nicklaus Academy of Golf at Grand Cypress Resort in Orlando, Florida, in 1985. Phil and I would teach several schools together, and our first golf school in January 1986 included Dick and Tom Smothers and Bill Murray. One of Phil's greatest attributes as a coach was his persistence in making sure the student successfully demonstrated what he was teaching them. A good example of this was in our first chipping session, and Bill Murray didn't adhere to Phil's chipping method. An important part of Phil's method was to eliminate the wrist by locking the club against the lead arm. After several unsuccessful attempts to get Bill to stop flipping his wrist, Phil asked for some duct tape. He took the tape and wrapped the club against Bill's forearm. Bill didn't even flinch. He continued to hit chip shots and eventually kept the club taped to his arm while eating lunch at the clubhouse.

Another of Phil's positive attributes was his willingness to help young teachers and talented aspiring players to get better at what they do. He would meet with us before his school started or during his lunch hour while sitting in a golf cart eating a boxed lunch and even after the school ended. You could sense the willingness and effort he would give to all of us who were fortunate to be mentored by Phil. Phil was certainly a guru when it came to his craft, but he had a big heart and a love for helping others. His influence on all of us will be lifelong. As a tribute to Phil, I am encouraged to keep his memory alive by being generous with my time in helping others.

(Left to right): Phil Rodgers, Fred Griffin and Jack Nicklaus. This picture was taken during the grand opening of the East Course at the Grand Cypress Resort, November 1985. Photo courtesy Fred Griffin.

Phil Rodgers and Fred Griffin.
Photo courtesy Fred Griffin.

Fred Griffin is currently the owner of Fred Griffin Golf at the Rosen Shingle Creek Resort, Orlando, Florida. He was named the North Florida PGA Teacher of the Year (1988/2019), *Golf Magazine* Top 100 Teachers in America, PGA National Finalist Teacher of the Year (2019), North Florida East Central Chapter Teacher of the Year (1988, 2009, 2019), *Golf Digest's* America's 50 Greatest Teachers, Golf Channel Academy Lead Coach (2015-2019) and *Golf Digest* Best Teachers in the State of Florida (2009-2022).

My Memories of Phil…

"FEARLESS"

by

Dr. Ralph Mann

President of CompuSport

Grand Cypress Academy of Golf (1986-2000)

I've worked with a number of elite coaches, and I can tell you that they are radically different from the average coach. They are also, unfortunately, very few in number. In my experience, there are four characteristics that make these individuals different.

First, and most importantly, they have a genetically gifted ability to understand their sport, at the highest level, and determine an athlete's strengths and weaknesses. This is something that cannot be taught. Second, they have the ability to maintain an athlete's strengths and, more importantly, improve their weaknesses. Third, toward the end of their careers, they always strive to better understand their sport, regardless of their age. Like the best athletes, they are always trying to get better. Finally, they are all fearless. The top athletes in every major sport make a lot of money. Thus, it takes a coach who is fearless to drive them to the top of their profession. It takes even more courage to make changes to an athlete's performance when they are at the top of their sport.

Thirty-seven years ago, Phil Rodgers was one of the first elite golf coaches that I encountered. For almost 20 years, I had the privilege of watching him work with golfers who ranged from beginners to the best in the world.

As a sports biomechanist, my job at the Jack Nicklaus Golf Academy was to provide the teachers with science-based information on the golf swings of our students in real time, during the actual lesson. To accomplish this took years of research, an elaborate video and computer system, a computer program with a million lines of code and a full-time computer operator. Phil had the uncanny ability to identify the same strengths and weaknesses of his students before we had the chance to provide our analysis. More importantly, he had the insight to determine which of these weaknesses to work on to get the most improvement, which is something that we could not provide.

Determining a golfer's strengths and weaknesses is relatively easy compared to the challenge of improving the characteristics. The process of going from understanding what to teach to the difficult task of how to effectively teach is a rare skill in coaching. Once he had the list of teaching goals, Phil was unsurpassed in his ability to achieve results. In addition, his solutions were different depending on the skill level of the student. So, if a beginner and a tour player had the same problem, Phil's instruction would be decidedly different. He properly realized that there was a major difference between the physical and mental ability of a typical student and those of an elite tour player and adjusted his teaching to accommodate these differences.

Back in 1986 when I first met Phil, science was not a major factor in sport, and most established (older) coaches were either skeptical or outright hostile to the concept. Those coaches who realized that science could provide additional insight into their understanding of their sport were the ones who benefited the most. Like all great coaches, Phil had a big ego, but he never let it get in the way of improving his understanding of the game of golf.

I participated in numerous of Phil's lessons with PGA and LPGA TOUR players. Regardless of the player's level of success, Phil was relentless and expected every player to make the changes that he was confident would improve their performance. Unlike most coaches who work with elite athletes and are terrified that they may ruin a player's performance, Phil was fearless in his belief that what he saw in a player's swing could always lead to improvement. The opportunity to watch Phil and Jack Nicklaus on the practice tee, discussing (and sometimes arguing about) changes in either the full swing or short game mechanics is perhaps the best experience in my professional career.

When you take these impressive teaching skills and add Phil's playing ability (especially in the short game), you can see why Phil was a unique individual. After all these years, I still use him as my benchmark standard to judge coaches in every sport.

Davis Love III, Phil Rodgers and Dr. Ralph Mann.
Photo courtesy of Kevin McKinney.

Dr. Ralph Mann is currently the president of CompuSport in Bend, Oregon. He is a three-time NCAA champion in track and field at Brigham Young University. In 1972, he was a silver medalist in the Olympics in the 400-meter-high-hurdles. He also co-wrote the book *Swing Like a Pro: The Breakthrough Scientific Method of Perfecting Your Golf Swing* with Fred Griffin. In 2015, he was inducted into the USA National Track and Field Hall of Fame.

My Memories of Phil...

"Couldn't be Rattled"

by

Kevin McKinney

Former Sales Manager, Instructor and Range Attendant

Grand Cypress Academy of Golf (1985-1996)

Imagine it's the spring of 1986 and you're working as a range attendant at the first-ever Jack Nicklaus Academy of Golf, newly opened at Grand Cypress Resort in Orlando. The dean of instruction is a legendary tour player, close friend and fellow competitor of Jack Nicklaus. He's also a tough-minded former Marine known for his brash style. Philamon Webster Rodgers, or Phil as he was known to all, would fly to Orlando from La Jolla, California, and teach a series of popular three-day golf schools for amateurs of all abilities. Class starts early and, while you haven't met Phil yet, it's time to carry his bag full of Cobra clubs that bear his name to the lesson area and get to work. You're armed with chalk paint, tees, a bucket of balls and the sobering realization you're responsible for setting up his chipping presentation. There are special measurements scribbled on a small piece of paper, handed to you by a junior instructor. "Make sure you get it right," you are told. Easy to say you want to make a good impression on Phil while hiding mild terror of making a mistake. With students from all over the country seated around him, Phil demonstrates his tour-tested skills from the edge of the putting green. For each club, 6 iron through wedge, he knows exactly how far the ball should fly and roll, what he calls the air-to-ground ratio. His precision with these irons was amazing, just as good as the putter.

Phil demonstrating his chipping technique.
Photo courtesy of Kevin McKinney.

The presentation begins, and as fate would have it, the first shot comes up short... and that booming voice of the former Marine is quickly directed your way. You, the rookie range attendant, got the math wrong. The students chuckle and feel glad it wasn't them. We loved Phil. Everyone did. Underneath that intimidating persona was a generous soul who cared deeply for the game. A gifted teacher, his intellect and dedication were always evident, and he never failed to go the extra mile for his students and the staff.

After class was a favorite time. We'd watch him practice; he had remarkable control of his ball flight. He took time to help us with our swing and share wisdom from his decades of viewing the game in his unique way. We were told he never lost an individual match while at the University of Houston. Walking up to the first tee, he'd ask his competitors, "Which one of you is playing for second?"

One of my favorite memories of Phil being Phil occurred during a presentation on bunker shots. "Swing three times harder, and always get out in one," he would tell his attentive students. As he took the class on a verbal and visual journey of the art of sand play, each shot would mirror the other, landing softly on a gentle slope and slowly rolling to the pin, many finding the bottom of the cup. With Phil wearing his trademark bucket hat that shielded his eyes from the sun and the eye-to-eye gaze of the students seated above him, one student from New York had a hard time holding back his ego and entered the danger zone by saying, "Why don't you go for the far pin? Obviously the short one is too easy." Everyone knew this fellow couldn't break 100, and now he was instant prey for a Phil comeback. There was silence, the air became electric, and no one wanted to be near the impending doom. Well, the bucket hat never tilted up, the rhythm of delivery and volume in Phil's voice remained exactly as before, only a slight change in stance as he continued to explain the theoretical concepts of proper sand strategy. The next ball flew 30 yards to the far pin and stopped dead on the flag. After that, with the bucket hat still tilted down, he resumed the shorter shot and continued dispensing wisdom. It was as if the question had never been asked. Phil was world-class, couldn't be rattled, and that guy never asked a question again.

Phil demonstrating his bunker technique wearing his bucket hat. Photo courtesy Kevin McKinney.

Kevin McKinney is now the owner/co-founder of Executive Golf Events in Raleigh, North Carolina.

My Memories of Phil...

"I SAVE THOSE COOKIES FOR THE GOOD PLAYERS"

by

Adrian Stills

Former PGA TOUR Player and Head Instructor

Grand Cypress Academy of Golf (1985/1988-2000)

I moved to Orlando, Florida, in 1982 to pursue my dream of playing on the PGA TOUR. I played on the mini tours for a few years but needed a place to work on my game, so I got a job working as a valet at the Villas of Grand Cypress in 1985. The golf facilities there were amazing and a perfect place for me to practice. In 1986, my dream came true! I went from parking cars for a living to playing against the best players in the world on the PGA TOUR after qualifying through Q-School at Grenelefe Golf and Tennis Resort in Haines City, Florida. Like many rookies on the PGA TOUR, I was unable to retain my card after my first year and was forced to go back to the drawing board. Although there were some high moments that year, including qualifying for the U.S. Open at Shinnecock Hills Golf Club, I knew my game would need more work.

In 1988, my dream to play on the PGA TOUR was still alive. I applied for another job at Grand Cypress; however, this time I was working at the Academy of Golf. It was at the academy that I met Fred Griffin, Dr. Ralph Mann, Phil Rodgers, Gary Smith and a slew of amazing instructors. I will never forget the grand opening of the Jack Nicklaus-designed East Course. Fred, Phil and Jack held a press conference that day, played the East nine in front of the gallery, and later, Phil hosted a short game clinic on the sixth hole. I hung on Phil's every word and stood in awe as he demonstrated flop shots with his patented "figure eight" swing off hard-panned lies.

Opening press conference for the East Course at the Grand Cypress Resort. (Left to right): Fred Griffin, Phil Rodgers, Jack Nicklaus, Hermon Vonhoff , Developer of Grand Cypress and Lee Lockhart, VP of Jack Nicklaus Golf Services. Photo courtesy of Fred Griffin.

I grew up in Pensacola, Florida, and remember watching Phil play in the Pensacola Open as a kid. I didn't have the opportunity to meet him that week, but that long-awaited introduction was about to change. I began assisting Phil during his many golf schools, and over time, we became good friends. Phil knew that I wanted to get back out onto the PGA TOUR, so he worked with me on all aspects of my game. Phil was so smart and often talked about his mentor, Paul Runyan. Phil stated that Runyan wanted to know how the human body worked and researched and consulted with doctors on how the body's movements and the golf swing worked together, a practice unheard of during Runyan's era. This biomechanical information influenced Phil's young life and would later define how he would teach the game as an adult.

In 1998, 12 years after my first appearance, I qualified for my second U.S. Open at the Olympic Club, in San Fransico, California. My longtime friend Lee Janzen and I played a practice round together days before the opening round. I beat Lee out of $40 that day and felt good about my game except for two reasons. The first was the thick rough around the greens. Although I had hit a lot of greens in regulation during the practice round with Lee, the rough was brutal! The second was my physical health. I wasn't feeling well and ended up playing the U.S. Open that week with tonsillitis. I met Phil at the practice green and said, "Pro, this rough around the greens is killing me and I feel terrible." I was also, understandably, nervous about playing in my second major. Phil couldn't help my sore throat, but he was about to give me the lesson of a lifetime, as several tour players stood and watched, hoping to pick up some words of wisdom.

Phil explained to me, "When you are hitting bunker shots, you want to set your hands lower at address to set the heel lower and the toe higher. This allows you to use more of the heel and bounce of the sand wedge to blast the sand. However, when you are hitting from this U.S Open rough, set your hands higher to get the heel higher and the toe lower. This allows you to use more of the bounce on the toe side of the sand wedge to get less resistance so the club will slide through the rough easier." V.J. Singh was standing beside us and said, "Why have you never told me about this information before, Pro?" Phil responded without hesitation, "I save those cookies for the good players!" We all started laughing, including V.J. Phil's sense of humor and delivery were always perfect and well-timed.

I missed the cut at the U.S. Open and saw Lee after my second round. Lee said to me, "You and Marie should stick around. I'm going to win this tournament." We did stick around for the weekend and were there to witness Lee hoist the trophy on Sunday after beating Payne Stewart. Lee collected a winner's check for $535,000, minus the 40 bucks he lost to me earlier that week.

In 2000, I left Grand Cypress to return to my hometown of Pensacola to be the general manager and head golf professional at the Osceola Golf Course. I also got involved with the First Tee Organization and hosted a clinic to raise money for the organization. PGA TOUR players Bubba Watson, Joe Durant, Heath Slocum, Stewart Cink and Lucas Glover all came out to support the First Tee Northwest Florida's Pro-Am. I also had a long drive champion, Chuck "the Hit Man" Hiter, come in for the event. I drove up to Prattville, Alabama, to pick Phil up after he had taught a golf clinic at the Country Club of Birmingham with my former Grand Cypress co-worker Eric Eshleman.

Phil gave the short game clinic and then sat back in a golf cart as the long drive champion hit shots. Phil watched with his eagle eye and, after several minutes, without any prompting got out of his golf cart and explained to the audience the similarities of the long driver's golf swing to the upper body movements of Major League Baseball's Mark McQuire. Once again, Phil's mind for sports movements and the lessons he learned from Paul Runyan came to the forefront. Phil's ability to break down high-level athletic movements and then translate them to the golf swing was unsurpassed and made a lasting impression on me as a teacher as well as a player.

Just prior to Phil's death, I flew to San Diego, California, to visit with Phil and his wife, Karen. We decided to meet for lunch at a local restaurant. I talked with Phil on the phone earlier that day and Phil said, "Adrian, I don't want you to be shocked when you see me, but I have lost a lot of weight. In fact, let's meet out for lunch because if you come to the house, we will not be there. We are going to the racetrack. I heard they were hiring jockeys at Santa Anita." Phil's sense of humor to the very end of his life was still as sharp as his eye for teaching and his heart for helping others.

In 2000, Adrian Stills moved to Prattville, Alabama, to be the director of instruction at the Robert Trent Jones Trail Capitol Hill Golf Course. In 2002, he became general manager and head golf professional at the Osceola Golf Course. He held that position for 19 years. In 2021, he became the director of parks and recreation for the city of Pensacola for a year and a half. Adrian retired in 2023 from his position after more than 20 years of service to the city of Pensacola. He continues to work as the founding executive director of the Northwest Florida Chapter of the First Tee. He was instrumental in starting a fundraising campaign with Joe Durant, Bubba Watson, Heath Slocum and Boo Weekley. Adrian is a co-founder, board member and now serves as tournament director and director of player development for the APGA. The Advocates Professional Golf Association was established in 2010 as a nonprofit organization with the mission to bring greater diversity to the game of golf. The APGA Tour Board of Directors works to accomplish this by hosting and operating professional golf tournaments, player development programs and mentoring programs and by introducing the game to inner-city youth.

My Memories of Phil…

"WE HAD ALWAYS BEEN FRIENDS"

by
Brenda Pfeifer
Former Sales Manager
Grand Cypress Academy of Golf (1985-2004)

After graduating from the University of Florida, I was seeking employment, and the Villas of Grand Cypress was hiring. The beautiful resort, located minutes from Disney World, was about to make its grand opening, so I applied for an administrative position at the Villas. After being hired, I soon transferred departments from the Villas to the newly formed Jack Nicklaus Academy of Golf headed by Fred Griffin.

My responsibilities were to help with the administrative duties for the golf academy, including booking golf schools, helping students with their room accommodations and restaurant reservations, as well as their welcome gifts. I was also a "mother hen" to all the instructors, sales staff and outside assistants. I loved meeting the students when they first arrived at the golf school. It was fun finally getting to put a name to a face after talking with them over the phone for months. Over time, many of the students would return to the academy on a repeat basis – many from all over the world. In many ways, we all became a large extended family.

My first interaction with Phil was in 1985, when he came in to train the instructors on his teaching methodology for his signature Phil Rodgers Golf School. When I met Phil for the first time, it was as if we had always been friends. When Phil entered the room, you knew it, and we always had so much fun together.

In 2004, I changed jobs and left Grand Cypress for the Omni Resort to be a sales manager. After working at the Omni a few years, I won an incentive trip to San Diego. I contacted Phil and his wife, Karen, to let them know that my husband, Rick, and I would be staying two extra days and wanted to see them. Phil and Karen spent two days showing us the San Diego area, including La Jolla, the Torrey Pines Golf Course and his beautiful home. Our visit was during the week of the PGA TOUR event, the Farmers Insurance Open, held at Torrey Pines. Wherever Phil took us, people would say, "Hey Pro!" Phil and Karen were the perfect hosts, and Rick and I felt like royalty tagging along with them over those two days. Phil was a wonderful man, and he loved showing us around town. San Diego was Phil's hometown, and he was proud to show it off!

Brenda Pfeifer is currently the senior sales manager at the Wyndham Grand Orlando Resort Bonnet Creek, Orlando, Florida.

My Memories of Phil...

"PAY IT FORWARD"

by

Lee Houtteman

Former Instructor

Grand Cypress Academy of Golf (1985-1997)

After playing golf at Michigan State University, I moved to Orlando to pursue my playing career on the Florida mini tours. In 1985, I started working at the Grand Cypress Resort in the bag room to help pay the bills as well as to have access to their amazing practice facilities. The resort had just opened, and the guests who arrived there were a who's who of famous athletes, movie stars and successful businessmen and businesswomen, all converging on Grand Cypress to play the beautiful 45 holes.

While working in the bag room, I had the opportunity to meet Phil Rodgers. I knew of Phil as a former PGA TOUR player but was also intrigued by the fact that he was one of the best teachers in the world and knew that he could help my game. Phil was like a rock star! He was bigger than life, and when he showed up to teach his three-day golf school, people took notice. After all, he had just helped the one-and-only Jack Nicklaus win two majors in 1980 and the Masters in 1986.

I felt a little intimidated at first meeting Phil, but over time he warmed up to me and knew me by name. When I transitioned over from the bag room to start teaching at the Academy of Golf, Phil would come over and watch me hit some balls. I was amazed at his generosity to give of his time after teaching all day long. Phil was so generous with his time to all the instructors, and whenever he was teaching, we would all stand there and watch. His influence on my life has affected me in more ways than just teaching. Because of Phil Rodgers, I try to help other young PGA apprentices trying to make their way up the corporate ladder. When I see one of them out on the range trying to improve their game, I often think of Phil, walk over to them and help them with their game. In reality, I would rather just go home to be with my family, but, in life, sometimes you have to pay it forward and remember those who did the same for you. Thank you, Phil, for paying it forward to me!

Lee Houtteman is currently the director of golf at the Leland Country Club in Leland, Michigan. He is the Northern Michigan Teacher of the Year (2005) and Northern Michigan Player of the Year (2008). Lee is the two-time Michigan Senior PGA Player of the Year (2012/2018) and was inducted into the Northern Michigan PGA Hall of Fame (2013).

My Memories of Phil...

"UNCLE PHIL"

by

Joey Hidock

Former CompuSport Technician and Instructor

Grand Cypress Academy of Golf (1987-2009)

I started at the Grand Cypress Academy of Golf in 1987 working as a CompuSport technician. We used a computer software teaching system called ModelGolf (now SwingModel). Part of our job as technicians was to first build a model based on a student's body dimensions. We would then superimpose the model over the student's recorded swing and compare that swing to the model's golf swing. The model's swing was based on 54 PGA TOUR players' swings, including Jack Nicklaus, Tom Kite and Greg Norman. The model and the video teaching system, developed by Dr. Ralph Mann, gave both the instructor and the student great visual feedback about where the swing should be, starting with the set-up going all the way through to the finishing position.

Phil was not computer-savvy, but he was very interested in the software technology Dr. Mann had developed, so he would often watch the computer lessons and give his feedback. Over time, we became great friends, and I looked at him, as did all the instructors, like he was a part of the family. I felt it was disrespectful just to call him Phil or even Mr. Rodgers, so I started calling him "Uncle Phil."

None of the other instructors called him "Uncle Phil," so, in many ways, the two of us had a special bond. I thought of him as more than just an instructor; he was an overall great guy. Uncle Phil cared deeply about all of our golf games but, more importantly, he cared about us as people. At Grand Cypress, he was the king – a man who would often take out a $100 bill and send me to Taco Bell to buy lunch for all the instructors. My time spent with Uncle Phil at Grand Cypress is a time of my life I will never forget. He affected my life in so many ways. Uncle Phil was a fun and knowledgeable mentor to us all.

Great times with Uncle Phil.
Photo Courtesy of Joey Hidock.

Joey Hidock is currently a lead instructor at the Villages Golf Academy in The Villages, Florida. He received the Player Development Award (2018 and 2024) and the President's Award (2001) from the North Florida Section. He was named among *Golf Digest* Best Teachers in the State of Florida (2009-2013) and U.S. Kids Top 50 Instructor and established a PGA-endorsed program called "Putting on Smiles," where he putts at hospitals with children suffering with cancer.

My Memories of Phil…

"THANK YOU, PRO!"

by

Todd Meena

Former Head Instructor

Grand Cypress Academy of Golf (1988-2018)

I had heard of Phil Rodgers and his invaluable help to Jack Nicklaus' revamped short game as a new hire on the teaching staff at the Jack Nicklaus Academy of Golf at Grand Cypress. However, I knew very little of the man. That was about to change, and with it, so was the direction of my professional life. I had absolutely no idea the wild ride I was about to embark on alongside six other blessed souls (instructors) who would get the education of a lifetime simply by being in the right place at the right time.

I had no idea how poignant my first interaction with Phil would be, and, looking back, it capsulized my many fond and cherished memories of him. I was hitting bunker shots at the academy's par-4 practice hole. This was not a particularly strong part of my golf game, so when I noticed Phil approaching to watch me hit a few bunker shots, my heart started to race. We hadn't even met yet, but there he was, driving up in a cart to check out the new guy. This was going to be a disaster, I thought. Could I get fired for incompetence on my second day? He stopped and watched without saying a word. There was nothing left for me to do but hit what was assuredly going to be a shank or skulled shot. In a half-fainting state of semi-coma, I proceeded. Somehow, by God's grace, my ball came to rest three feet from the hole. To this day, I consider it the luckiest shot I have ever hit, as I had absolutely no control over what I was doing.

Totally relieved, I found the courage to look up at the man in the cart. In a gruff voice that I can only describe as something you would hear from a salty sea captain, Phil groaned "THAT'S TERRRRIBLE!" I was stupefied and speechless. Fortunately, he continued, "You'll never make any with the ball junk spinning to the right like that!" "What! Who is this guy?" I thought to myself.

Well, this guy, Phil Rodgers, proceeded to spend the next hour with someone he didn't even know and introduced me to "hooking" my bunker shots to create more height and cure me of my dreaded slice spin that my previous bunker technique embodied. He taught me how to release the club better than I knew I could and improved my bunker game immediately.

There were many other lessons that my colleagues and I were privileged to learn from "Pro" – the title bestowed upon Phil Rodgers with reverence. He habitually would take time after teaching an all-day golf school to help those mentoring under him. These were lessons for a lifetime that he gave to us for free. He just wanted to see us succeed. He had one of the biggest hearts I have ever known, and for as long as I live, I will never forget the sound of his club hitting sand or the image of his hands barely holding the club after making the sound. Thank you, Pro!

Todd Meena is currently the teaching professional at The Club at Bella Collina in Montverde, Florida. Todd has been ranked as a *Golf Digest* Best Teachers in the State of Florida on multiple occasions and was named the Grand Cypress Employee of the Year (1993 and 2005).

My Memories of Phil…

"Soft Hands"

by

Doug Lowen

Former Head Instructor/Instructor

Grand Cypress Academy of Golf (1988-2019)

I started at Grand Cypress in 1988 picking the driving range after moving to Orlando from Hays, Kansas. I was playing professionally on the Space Coast Mini Tour and knew that working at the Academy of Golf would allow me the opportunity to work on my game as well as learn how to teach. I remember one of the first times meeting Phil Rodgers. One evening, I was closing the driving range; I was tired and ready to go home. Suddenly, Phil drove up in his golf cart and asked if I wanted to go out and play a quick nine holes with two other instructors – Adrian Stills and Lee Houtteman. I said, "I would love to, but I'm closing the range, so I can't play today." Phil could see the disappointment on my face.

The next day, Phil asked me again. I was able to join Phil, Lee and Adrian in a money game on the North Course at Grand Cypress. Phil hit the ball everywhere that day and only hit three greens in regulation, but incredibly shot 3 under par! He made birdies on all three holes that he hit in regulation and got up-and-down six out of six times. Nearly all his up-and-downs were conceded putts, due to the fact that the putts were less than a foot from the hole. Those nine holes were my introduction to Phil's amazing short game.

Phil could take a baffler wood, which is comparable to a hybrid by today's standard, bury the ball into the sand in a greenside bunker and pop the ball out every time to a close pin. His teaching eye was world-renowned. Phil rarely needed video while teaching, but when he did use it, the video always verified what he had seen.

When I think of Phil teaching a golf school or playing on the golf course, I can still see his soft hands holding the club. He never forced the swing in the short game, and his touch and control were the best I have ever seen.

Doug Lowen is currently a PGA member and Junior Instructor at the Heathrow Country Club in Orlando, Florida. He played collegiately at Fort Hays State University and currently plays in the North Florida PGA section events.

My Memories of Phil...

"You Had to Miss the Green"

by

Kevin Weeks

Former Range Attendant/Dupont Coordinator

Grand Cypress Academy of Golf (1988-95)

In 1987, I graduated from Ole Miss after playing there under my coach, Ernest Ross. After graduation, I knew I wanted to teach golf, so I reached out to Coach Ross for advice. Coach Ross had a college roommate who was his teammate and knew Jack Nicklaus. Coach Ross called his former teammate, and he called Jack to get me an entry-level job working in the bag room at the Grand Cypress Resort. Brad Doyle, the former director of golf for the Grand Cypress Pro Shop, would always laugh when recounting my job hire because I showed up in a suit and tie for a bag room position and Jack Nicklaus was my reference. After starting in the bag room, I eventually worked my way over to the Academy of Golf, where I was hired by Fred Griffin to be a range attendant for the golf schools.

The first time I met Phil Rodgers, I was practicing bunker shots at the academy on my day off from work. I was using my Cobra Trusty Rusty wedges and felt the presence of someone standing behind me. I hit a shot and then turned around, and the man who designed the Trusty Rustys was standing in front of me. Phil stepped down into the bunker and looked at my wedges. He then took the time to give me some advice. Weeks later, before Phil headed back to California, new wedges arrived addressed to yours truly. Unbeknownst to me, Phil had called Cobra and had a set of his new wedges shipped.

One day after work, Phil asked me if I wanted to go play nine holes with him on the East Course at Grand Cypress. I said, "Sure, I would love to!" Phil said, "Ok, here is the game. You have to miss the green in regulation." I had never played that game before but was ready for the challenge. I played really well that day and shot 38, 2 over par. Phil shot 35, 1 under par. He chipped in twice and made one bogey. I learned a lot that day about the short game and how to manage it. I often play this game with my students to make short-game practice fun as well as a learning experience.

What I remember most about Phil was his big heart. If you worked hard, he wanted to help you. I try to pass this on to all my students. The students who put in the time and work the hardest get more of my time during clinics. Phil was the best, and the time he spent mentoring me and his encouragement helped me to become the teacher I am today.

Kevin Weeks is currently the director of instruction at Cog Hill Golf and Country Club in Lemont, Illinois. He was named the 2023 National PGA Teacher of the Year. He was named the Illinois Section Teacher of the Year (2005, 2007, 2009). He has been named a *Golf Magazine* Top 100 Teacher and *Golf Digest* Top 50 Teacher, as well as among the *Golf Digest* Best Teachers in the State of Illinois, ranking No. 1 in the state (2016-2024).

My Memories of Phil…

"PHIL BLESSED ALL OF US…"

by

Gus "The General" Holbrook

Former Head Instructor

Grand Cypress Academy of Golf (1989-2019)

I met Phil Rodgers in 1989 at Grand Cypress. He was teaching golf schools part time while juggling his teaching career, life on the Senior PGA TOUR and his home life in San Diego. Phil taught between 10 to 15 three-day schools per year, and I was fortunate enough to teach the majority of them with him. Before meeting Phil, I thought I knew a decent amount about the short game. I wasn't even close to this guy. I would sit and listen to his presentations while taking notes – pages and pages of notes over the years and then go home and take more notes on his interaction with his students. Phil wanted me to know you can't teach everyone the same way. Phil had the ability to teach the same swing move 10 different ways to get the needed results for his student. The definition of a great professor or instructor is to take something complex and make it simple, whether it be a math problem or a golf swing move. Phil checked all the boxes.

Over time, Phil and I got to be close friends through the cocktail parties held the night before the golf schools and the dinners afterward, almost always at Morton's Steak House with a group of four to six of us. The stories he told were classic. I was instructing in all the Dupont Golf Schools, which consisted of morning instruction and playing with the students in the afternoon. It also consisted of cocktail parties after each afternoon round of golf and then dinner. We would go to the best restaurants on property – Hemingway's, Black Swan or White Horse Saloon. All were great. I talked to the "powers that be" at DuPont to put Phil in the schools as a guest instructor. HE STOLE THE SHOW! He interacted with the students with his humor and more great stories, but more importantly to me, I got to watch him teach! Boy, did I learn a lot and took even more notes.

I have hundreds of stories about Phil, but one of my favorites was when a young Phil Rodgers was playing in the Masters as an amateur, and the great Ben Hogan took him under his wing for the week. In one of the practice rounds, Ben was showing Phil how to get the ball to Sunday's pin placements, actually hitting the ball to those exact positions. After the round, Ben got beat out of $5 by one of the other guys in the group. Under his breath, Ben frustratedly said, "I can beat that guy with just my irons!" Phil responded, "You probably could have, but you were playing to Sunday's pin placements, and today is Tuesday." That story is a classic.

About five years before Phil died, roughly 15 academy staff members got together with Phil for dinner – steak, of course. As the evening was ending, I got up and gave a toast to our friend and said, "May God bless Phil Rodgers because Phil blessed all of us." About five days before Phil died, he called me. We talked for a few minutes, and I could tell he was struggling. I asked, "Are you Ok?" He responded, "No. I'm in hospice. I wanted to call you to say goodbye." It was a tough phone call. I miss my friend. I love you buddy! Thanks for the memories!

Gus Holbrook is currently a teaching professional at the Barnsley Gardens Resort and Coosa Country Club in Rome, Georgia. He was a *Golf Digest* Best Teachers in the State of Florida (1996-2019). Gus was an All-American (1977) at the University of Georgia and was teammates with Chip Beck, Griff Moody and Tim Simpson. He was a two-time All-Southeastern Conference player (1977,1978). He represented the United States in 1977 on an all-star team that competed in Japan against a Japanese all-star team. The American team included his two-man partner, John Cook, Scott Hoch, David Edwards, Chip Beck, Lindy Miller and Joe Walter.

My Memories of Phil…

"FUN TIMES WITH PHIL"

by

Harry Zimmerman

Head Instructor

Grand Cypress Academy of Golf (1989-2019)

When I think of Phil, I am reminded of several funny stories that happened while teaching with him during his golf school at Grand Cypress. The first story was about one of our students, Steve, who was from New York. Steve came to the Phil Rodgers Golf School and was wearing white high-top sneakers that he had painted red. Phil was demonstrating to the students how to hit his patented flop shot over a deep bunker. Phil had gotten some brand-new wedges from Cobra and was trying them out for the first time as the students sat and watched. Suddenly, Steve got out of his chair and started swinging Phil's sand wedge that was fresh out of the wrapper while Phil was demonstrating the flop shot technique. Phil didn't notice that Steve was out of his chair, and, as Phil was taking his backswing, the club Steve was swinging hit

Phil's club in mid-swing and put a huge dent into the back of his brand-new sand wedge. Needless to say, Phil was not happy.

Another memorable story was when Phil was teaching an all-day school. Phil was demonstrating how to hit a bunker shot, and one of the students chimed in, "I bet you a drink you can't get it within five feet of the hole." I laughed and said to myself, "That's not a smart bet." Phil hit a beautiful shot right beside the hole. The student immediately responded, "Double or nothing you can't do that again." Phil hit another spectacular shot beside the hole. The student said, "Double or nothing again!" I laughed to myself and thought, "This guy is a glutton for punishment." Phil hit it inside five feet a third and final time as his defeated student shook his head in disbelief. That night, Phil went to dinner and saw his student sitting at the bar. Drinks were flowing that evening, and Phil was a wee bit late the next day for the early morning golf school. There certainly was never a dull moment when Phil Rodgers was teaching a golf school.

Harry Zimmerman is currently a PGA teaching professional at the Marriott Grande Vista Golf Academy in Orlando, Florida. He was named the North Florida East Central Chapter Teacher of the Year (2000) and was also named *Golf Digest* Best Teachers in the State of Florida (2006-2019).

My Memories of Phil...

"PRO AND HIS COOKIES"

by

Carl Alexander

Former Instructor

Grand Cypress Academy of Golf (1991-1999)

I met Phil when I started working at the Grand Cypress Academy of Golf in 1992. I knew of him from his reputation, but until I saw Phil coach firsthand, I knew nothing. To see "Pro" teach a golf school was something to behold. I watched him get results from students I thought had no chance to improve. Sometimes the results came from a quick fix, and sometimes they came from a major change. He would stalk around each player without speaking for a bit and then yell out, "Better!" or a simple, "No, that's not it." It was unlike any golf coaching I'd seen before. It was more like my high school soccer coach than the professionals I was around at Westchester Country Club. But his brash style got results, and I was both curious and in awe.

Phil was incredibly kind and giving of his time once you had gained his respect. He had to like you and respect you before he would share any of his "coaching cookies." With his experience from being an elite amateur and PGA TOUR player to teaching top players, Phil was one of the best in the business. I was privileged to see him coach PGA TOUR players like Davis Love III, Seve Ballesteros and many others.

Phil was hands on with a young Davis Love III.
Photo courtesy of Kevin McKinney.

My favorite memories were when Phil was in a bunker, slapping at the sand and hitting all kinds of shots out of the bunker. From the clubface wide open to clubface closed, ball forward and ball back, cut across it or loop it in a figure-eight hook swing, Phil had all the bunker shots and always carried a bag full of his "Trusty Rusty" wedges that he had designed. Phil loved competition and would challenge anyone willing to take him on in a wedge contest.

After watching one of Phil's chipping presentations, I took some of his wedges, along with my friend Harold Wyatt, to the Grand Cypress maintenance facility to grind our wedges like the "Trusty Rusty" wedges. Phil was big into grinding the sole of his wedges so you could lay the face open, and the bounce wouldn't lift the leading edge up off the ground too high. He wanted you to hit the heel of the wedge into the turf, and turf interaction was a key to Phil's concept of good wedge play.

We grabbed his wedges and took ours and drove to the maintenance facility where they had a circular grinding stone. We held up his wedge as our model while grinding ours. We tried to make our wedges look the same as his wedges and thought we did well, until we returned. Phil let us know that we had just ruined our new wedges. However, Phil loved our effort and later gave us a few of his "cookies" for wedge design.

One of his "cookies" was regarding the club face. Phil didn't want too much club outside the scoring lines on the toe, and the sweet spot had to line up with the dead center of the club face. He wanted the leading edge straighter than most wedges. He also wanted the maximum bounce possible for some shots, so you could hit down into the ground as hard as you could. Phil could also reduce the bounce by squaring the clubface to pinch the ball and stop it with more spin. He was a master at both wedge design and the execution of any wedge shot. His presentations were animated, entertaining and impressive, and I regret that I never filmed an entire presentation.

I fell in love with teaching at the Grand Cypress Academy of Golf. Dr. Mann, Fred Griffin and Phil Rodgers were the spark that lit my coaching fire. Teaching and working with an outstanding team of PGA professionals set the groundwork for where I am today. The academy offered numerous golf schools per week, with up to 16 players per school. Some of our students were difficult, and Phil would battle with them. He wouldn't ignore or avoid them like other professionals might. He would get right in there and break them down to see it his way and improve. If needed, he would tell a student "That's not it. That's terrible." His tough love was direct, sincere and showed he cared.

Phil loved fly fishing, his other passion. He would often relate the loading of the club shaft and the release of that energy into the golf ball as a similar motion to throwing a fly cast. He referred to it as "load and snap it."

Phil was a tremendous help with my own game. He would sit quietly in a cart or stand up and pace around watching me and the other instructors hitting balls. He talked less than most teaching professionals, but the words he used were powerful and impactful. Phil's way of explaining the golf swing was very visual. He would grab you and your club and try to get you to feel what he was describing. You knew he was 100% into it when he was teaching you.

Phil's career as a professional golfer was impressive, but the impact he has had on professional golfers and coaches around the world is more important. He was a father figure to many of us, and he cared about how we were playing and progressing in our careers. To this day, I meet professionals who were affected by their time with Phil and how he helped them with their game or their coaching. He helped build the Cobra brand and designed clubs that have been copied by other companies. He was a legend in the game, and I am forever grateful for his mentorship.

Phil had an amazing life, and if you were lucky enough to go to dinner with him, you would enjoy some nice wine while he would hold court. He told amazing stories about galivanting around Manhattan with Joe Namath and Mickey Mantle until the sun came up. He talked about growing up, learning from Paul Runyan and playing with Ben Hogan, Arnold Palmer, Jack Nicklaus and other legends in the game. The instructors would ask him a million questions until he got tired of it and would say, "That's it boys. Time to go." But then the next day, he would spend his lunch hour watching us hit balls and helping us get better. His impact on the game of golf and the lives of the many professionals he has touched has been impressive. We are forever grateful!

Phil and Carl at the Grand Cypress Academy of Golf.
Photo courtesy of Carl Alexander.

Carl Alexander is currently the director of golf at the Golf Club of Purchase in Purchase, New York. He is the National Horton Smith Award winner for the PGA of America (2012) and the Metropolitan Teacher of the Year (2006). Carl is also recognized by Golf Digest as Best Teachers in the State of New York (2013-2023).

My Memories of Phil…

"PHIL HAD THEIR FULL ATTENTION"

by

Eric Eshleman

Former Head Instructor

Grand Cypress Academy of Golf (1992-1997)

I got my start in the golf business in 1992 working at the Grand Cypress Academy of Golf. The golf school business was booming, so I quickly went from picking the driving range to getting my instructor certification and teaching students alongside an amazing staff in no time. I vividly remember teaching golf schools with Phil Rodgers. During the winter months of the mid '90s, travelers from the Northeast would converge on Orlando to escape the snow and cold to take in some golf instruction and play the 45-hole golfing oasis. Tee times were packed, and instruction books were full, making it the perfect place for a new instructor to get started.

The Phil Rodgers Golf Schools were always full of eager students looking to get better. The majority of the students were "type A" personalities fresh off Wall Street who would fly in on Thursday and depart Sunday. They would gorge themselves on golf instruction and practice and play from sunup to sundown. On the first day of golf school, the students would drive down to the academy just after breakfast. Waiting on them there was a row of chairs in the shape of a semi-circle, a pyramid of golf balls for each student and their golf bags, neatly organized on a bag stand in front of an immaculate short-game area. I can still see the beauty of the resort on those cool winter mornings at sunrise as the dew started to burn off the perfectly mowed fairways and the steam rose from the nearby ponds that surrounded the academy.

As the students anxiously sat and waited to watch Phil's presentation, he would look at me and say, "Eric, I think I'm going after cart No. 3 today." The students would then look at each other in bewilderment as Phil would open the face of his lob wedge and hit his patented flop shot up into the air and, nine times out of 10, land it on the top of the third cart's roof. At that moment, Phil had their full attention.

Years later, my wife and I moved to Birmingham, Alabama, where my career path led me to the Country Club of Birmingham. In 2001, I had Phil come to Birmingham to host a golf school for our membership. At the time, Kelli was nine months pregnant with our eldest son, Ryan. There are two things I loved about Phil. One was his sense of humor and the other was his passion for food and good wine. Phil loved to indulge in the finer things in life, and, over the years he had gained a few extra pounds around the waistline. His running joke to the students was, "I'm getting so old that my muscles hurt, so I'm letting my muscles turn to fat. My fat doesn't hurt!" Phil thought it would be great if he and Kelli would have a picture taken side by side with both their bellies touching so people could guess who was the one in the picture that was nine months pregnant.

Kelli and Phil touching bellies!
Photo courtesy Kelli Eshleman.

Phil's ability to laugh at himself was evident in 1998 when I attended the PGA Teaching Summit in New Orleans, Louisiana. The summit was held inside the New Orleans Superdome, and Phil was doing a bunker presentation early in the morning with Butch Harmon. Phil was not loose and got into the bunker they had created on a huge stage, while thousands of PGA golf professionals eagerly sat to watch his demonstration. Phil and Butch were both hooked up to wireless mics. I'm sure the two of them had enjoyed a wonderful dinner the night before with some very expensive wine. Phil got into the bunker and dead-skulled it out of the bunker, flying the golf ball into the stadium seats, almost hitting a cleaning lady who was vacuuming the floors. Most teachers would have wanted to crawl under the stage, but not Phil. Both he and Butch laughed hysterically, proving that even the best players in the world hit poor shots, especially when they are not warmed up.

Phil had the best teaching eye I have ever seen. Most instructors, especially new ones, rely on video to see the problems in a golf swing, especially for the elite players on the PGA TOUR. One day while I was watching Phil hit balls at Grand Cypress, I was talking with Curtis Cowen, one of our CompuSport technicians who worked under Dr. Mann. Curtis was informing Phil while he was hitting balls about all the new video cameras the academy was purchasing. The new cameras all had high-speed shutters, allowing the instructors to have perfect video quality for their students, frame by frame. Phil hit a shot and turned to Curtis and pointed to his eyes and then showed him his hands and said, "Nothing you got is as good as these!" Curtis and I both laughed because we both knew he was right. The camera might show the fault, but the camera can't fix the problem.

Phil Rodgers touched my life in so many ways both as a teacher and as a golf professional. One of the two things I remember most about him was that as much as he pushed his students with his Marine-like persistence, or the rare times he hit a poor shot on the course when we would play, or whenever we went to dinner with all the other instructors where the language sometimes got loose, I never once heard him curse. The second thing I remember and try my best to emulate is that Phil would work all day teaching his students and then come over and help me and the other instructors with our own games. His example of sharing his knowledge with the next generation of teachers is the benchmark for how all PGA golf professionals should mentor to grow the game today.

Eric Eshleman is currently the director of golf at the Country Club of Birmingham in Birmingham, Alabama. In 2021, he was elected to the Board of Directors for the PGA of America. He was awarded the National Golf Professional of the Year for the PGA of America (2019) and was named the Teacher of the Year for the Alabama- Northwest Florida Section (2004/2010). Eric was a *Golf Digest* Best Teachers in the State of Alabama (2000-2023).

My Memories of Phil...

"THE OLD PRO"

by

Harold Wyatt

Former Caddie for Phil Rodgers and Golf School Assistant

Grand Cypress Academy of Golf (1991-1994)

I met Phil Rodgers in January of 1991 after graduating from the University of Georgia. I moved to Orlando to pursue a career as a professional golfer. My job was to set up the golf schools and assist Phil and the team of teaching professionals. I had heard about Phil from the teaching pros and was aware of the influence and instruction he provided Jack Nicklaus to resurrect his career in 1980. Phil's introduction was not warm and fuzzy, and I'd expect most who meet him for the first time would echo the same. He was slow to speak, observant, serious, gruff and standoffish. Of course, I later came to learn that "The Old Pro," as we called him, was nothing like that first impression. He was gregarious, funny and, to use some Southern vernacular, a total "cut-up" who loved clowning around. He loved to verbally spar with anyone who was capable, and he loved life. But what he loved most was teaching.

Phil was a San Diego native, the individual NCAA champion at the University of Houston, a Marine and a five-time PGA

TOUR winner. He recorded his first professional win at the L.A. Open in January of 1962, which ironically, was Jack Nicklaus' first tournament as a professional. Jack and Phil were essentially the same age, and both played in the Masters as amateurs. They famously ate multiple Chateaubriand steaks nightly at Augusta National that year while staying together in the Crow's Nest. Meeting Phil Rodgers and then becoming a friend and student of his was by far the single most important event in my golf life. I was blessed to be one of his many "pupils," as he used to call us. I loved that term.

Phil had some early success on what was then called the Senior PGA TOUR. He turned 50 in April of 1988, and, by the time I arrived at Grand Cypress in early 1991, had refocused and was committed to competing in senior events when he wasn't teaching. In April of '91, he had held the lead and was in contention at The Tradition coming down the stretch. This was the first major of the year (then held in Arizona) and everyone at Grand Cypress was paying close attention. We gathered around the TV watching him play over the weekend and he ended up finishing in second place, to none other than Jack Nicklaus.

Phil adopted me soon thereafter (along with many other young players) and spent a lot of time sharing his sophisticated methods and techniques. A couple of years later, he asked me to temporarily fill in and caddie for him in the 1993 GTE Suncoast Classic. Phil, his lovely wife, Karen, and I all met in Tampa that week. The tournament happened to be Bob Murphy's first Senior PGA TOUR event, garnering a lot of media attention. Phil was paired with Murphy in the first round in one of the featured groups. Phil didn't play well that week and shot in the mid-70s each round, finishing well back in the pack. The course was difficult, and he wasn't sharp, making very few birdies. "The Old Pro" was off his game, and he wasn't happy with his performance. Plus, he had a rookie caddie who probably was burdensome in some ways, but it was a great experience to be with him inside the ropes. Phil was very generous with cash and a lot of golf balls as my compensation for the week. Several weeks later, I won my first professional golf tournament, which was both my first and last victory.

The experience all of us had with Phil was invaluable. He was great company, loved to eat and drink good wine. He loved to teach and have fun, and he was generous with his information, his experiences and his time. Phil didn't have kids, so the staff at Grand Cypress were his surrogate sons, and he loved us all. When Phil came to Grand Cypress for golf schools, we'd always have a big group from the academy go out to dinner, and Phil would hold court. Another interesting thing about Phil was that he also was big on living in the present and didn't like to look backward or think too much about the past. He and I had a few discussions about this over the years, and he always seemed to stress the importance of living in the present and looking forward.

Phil would also teach at the Country Club of Birmingham with the director of golf and former Grand Cypress work colleague, Eric Eshleman. Eric would occasionally let me know when Phil was in town. I'd meet them, and we'd practice some, have a meal and catch up. The last time I saw Phil in Birmingham, Hubert Green was there, and Phil was teaching Hubert, me and Eric together. It was very interesting listening to Phil instruct Hubert and then observe how Hubert, an 18-time TOUR winner and a two-time major champion, received his instruction. It was remarkable watching two aging pros who had enjoyed success at the top of their profession still grinding away and trying to get better, with Hubert listening intently. Phil was well-respected by all in the game, including the greats of the game.

Sometime in the early 2000s, Carl Alexander and I flew out to Los Angeles to play the L.A. Country Club, Riviera and Bel Air Country Club. We then drove south to play golf with Phil at La Jolla Country Club. La Jolla was where Phil had grown up playing and received the tutelage from Paul Runyan. It was quite a memorable trip playing golf on such great courses and reuniting with Phil on his California turf. We stayed in La Jolla for three days at Phil and Karen's home.

The "old pro" working with me and doing what he loved-teaching golf.

Phil took us out to Carlsbad to the Cobra factory, where we got to see the design and manufacturing team making the wedges he designed. We then went to the Titleist Performance Institute for a tour of that facility as well as a practice session. We wrapped up the trip with Sunday night NFL football with the Chargers playing the Raiders. Phil was good friends with Dean Spanos, who owned the Chargers, so we started the game on the field and then retired to the owner's box for the rest of the game. It was quite a luxurious treat, and we had a ball! Phil was such a great host, and the next day, Dean joined us for golf at La Jolla.

Phil had contracted leukemia years earlier, which affected him physically, but he was able to stabilize it with medication and live many good years after his initial diagnosis. He had lost a lot of distance and strength at that point but still had great technique and could still hit high-quality shots. Of course, Phil holed out a shot from about 140 yards and let us hear about it in his typically loud manner. That was my last round of golf with him.

To say Phil Rodgers had a big impact on me would be a huge understatement. Phil was my golf father in some ways and a friend, and I was blessed to have known him. He was extremely authentic, a real man, and what you saw was what you got. He loved his wife, Karen, and her family, and he loved his life and all the relationships that came with it.

After three years of playing on the mini tour circuit from 1991-1994, I accepted that my destiny was not the PGA TOUR. I moved back to Georgia and started a commercial real estate career in 1995. After three years, I was fully reinstated to amateur status and started competing regularly as an amateur, when time allowed. Although I "failed" as a professional golfer, it was one of the best experiences of my life pursuing that dream, and Phil Rodgers was an integral part of the experience.

I was fortunate to be able to have much greater success as an amateur golfer than I did as a pro. I qualified for two U.S. Amateurs, two U.S. Mid Amateurs and one British Amateur, and I enjoyed many other great performances in high-profile tournaments in Georgia and around the country. I was a medalist in qualifying for the 2004 U.S. Amateur, which was held at Winged Foot. Given Phil's experience in playing major championships at Winged Foot, I was able to consult with him during my preparations for the event. How many amateurs get to pick up the phone and ask questions of someone who's played in U.S. Opens at the same course? I'll never forget Phil's answer when I asked, "What's the key to playing Winged Foot?" Phil immediately barked at me over the phone, "Play to the middle third of the greens." I followed his instructions, and it almost worked, as I missed qualifying for the low-64 match play bracket by one shot.

In October of 2017, I attended an investment conference at Torrey Pines, so I called Phil to let him know I would be in town. I met Phil and Karen for dinner at a nice restaurant on the beach in La Jolla. It was a very pleasant evening catching up and reminiscing about past times. We spent most of the time talking about my kids, and he and Karen were very interested in all the details. He was very weak and moving very slowly, but his mind was still sharp. He treated me to dinner, had branzino, and like he always did, ordered us a fine wine. That evening was the last time I saw "The Old Pro" before he passed away on June 26, 2018.

A day with Phil at the Titleist Performance Institute, Carlsbad, California, 2005.

Photos courtesy of Harold Wyatt.

Harold Wyatt is currently the owner of Wyatt Capital, a commercial real estate investment firm in Atlanta, Georgia.

My Memories of Phil…

"LANDED IT ON A DIME"

by

Jason Bell

Former Instructor

Grand Cypress Academy of Golf (2000-2008)

I moved from Hays, Kansas, to Orlando, Florida, to pursue my dream to play professional golf on the mini tours. I knew to accomplish my goals I would need a place to practice, so I got a job working at the Grand Cypress Academy of Golf. The practice facilities were exactly what my game needed. I was hired to pick the driving range and was a school assistant. My job was to set up the golf schools for the instructors, assist the students if they needed anything, feed them more balls when the students ran out and make sure the practice greens were cleaned after each session.

I remember the first time I assisted a Phil Rodgers Short Game School. I had never met Phil and was unaware of his teaching style. Phil had just given his bunker presentation, and there was a guy in the school who had a big ego, thought he knew what he was doing on the golf course, but had very little game. The student, after only a few swings, said a profanity followed by, "This doesn't work!" Phil was helping another student and overheard the comment. He immediately replied, "That's because you're not doing what I told you to do! I want you to throw the sand over your left shoulder!"

Phil would often have students put sand on the clubface of their sand wedge, turn toward the target with no backswing and release the sand, making it fly over their left shoulder (if they were right-handed) to teach the proper release. Phil then walked over and, within a few minutes, completely broke the student's bunker swing down as well as his ego. Then I witnessed firsthand the magic of Phil's teaching style. Phil slowly built him back up! Phil's verbiage went from "No that's not it!" to "That's better! Do it again!"

I had never seen anything like it. I couldn't believe how quickly the student's bunker game improved. Once the student's ego had been broken down, he started improving and, by the end of the golf school, the student was hanging on Phil's every word.

Phil influenced me as a player as well. I remember watching him give his chipping presentation that he learned from his mentor, Paul Runyan. Phil would place a dime out on the green, and his ball would be located several yards off the green. He would say to the students, "This is the spot where I want to land the ball." I then stood there in awe as he hit the shot and the ball landed on the dime and slowly rolled to the hole. I couldn't believe it! I wanted to learn this system, so when I practiced, I put a towel on the green and struggled to land it on the towel, and yet Phil was landing it literally on a dime. I adopted his chipping method and added it into my own game.

Several years later, I was playing in a PGA sectional event and was in a playoff. My opponent and I both missed the green and both had long chip shots to the pin. I walked off my air-time and walked to the hole to get my roll-time. I was 60 feet from the hole, took out my 7-iron (a club I never would have taken out prior to meeting Phil) and landed the ball on the green, watching it roll inches from the pin. My opponent, who had a similar shot, took out a much more lofted club and barely got it onto the green. I won the tournament and said to myself on the drive home, "This chipping method really works!" It was the same system Phil had taught Jack Nicklaus in 1980.

But the thing I remember most about Phil was how much he cared about my game as well as the other instructors' games. Phil would take his own personal time to help me as a player and was always interested in my game, and for that, I will always be grateful. Years later, I transitioned to teaching full time and, after having watched Phil teach, said to myself, "This is how I want to teach. I want to teach like Phil Rodgers." But as all the instructors know who were blessed to learn from Phil, we can pass on the information he taught us, but there will never be another Phil Rodgers.

Jason Bell is currently a public insurance adjuster in Orlando, Florida. After leaving Grand Cypress, he taught Sam Horsfield on the European Tour for four years as well as at more than 20 PGA TOUR events, including the U.S. Open (2015, 2016, 2019 and 2022). Jason has been a PGA member since 2000.

My Memories of Phil…

"DON'T EVER FORGET IT!"

by

Blake Holbrook

Former Student of Phil Rodgers (1997-2004)

I was a freshman at Dr. Phillips High School in Orlando, Florida, trying out for the varsity golf team. I worked extremely hard to make the team but came up short. I was not very tall and didn't hit the ball very far. I met Phil Rodgers through my father, Gus Holbrook, while he was a head instructor at Grand Cypress. Phil said to me in his rough-toned voice, "Blaker, don't worry about that. We will make you the best short-game player on the team, and you will bypass everyone next year." Over the next year, Phil worked with me a lot on my entire game. I didn't know what to think, but I trusted him and went with it. For countless hours, he worked with me in the bunker and around the green. At one point, I thought my hands were going to start bleeding.

One late afternoon, I was in the bunker practicing with Phil. I must have hit 500 or more shots but was not feeling the release he was trying to get me to feel after impact. Phil said in a loud voice, "Blaker, we will turn on the lights out here if we have to until we get it right. We will stay out here all night!" Well, somewhere in between shots 500 and 700, I did it. Phil yelled, "That's it, son! Did you feel that? Did you hear it? Don't ever forget it!" That was Phil. He worked tirelessly with you until you did it his way, and then he reinforced his message by letting you know you did it perfectly.

The following year, I made the varsity team and was one of the top two players on the team with the lowest scoring average. Our team's home course was none other than Arnold Palmer's home course, the Bay Hill Country Club. It was a great course for me to play and practice on, improving all parts of my game. My junior year, I was recruited by Florida Southern College to play golf. Florida Southern was known for its fantastic golf program, and I accepted following my senior year. With the likes of Lee Janzen, Rocco Mediate, Marco Dawson, Jeff Klauk and others, the college laid the foundation for a great golf program. The Florida Southern men's golf team has won 13 national championships – the most in NCAA Division II history.

My senior year, we lost the NCAA Division II national championship by one stroke. After my collegiate golf career, I played on various mini tours with some success and went to PGA TOUR Q-School twice, missing my last year by a few strokes. Without Phil's help during my high school years, who knows if my game would have been good enough to play collegiately. God bless you, Phil! You will always be the BEST!

Blake Holbrook currently lives in Gastonia, North Carolina, where he has retained his amateur status playing at the Gastonia Country Club. From 2012 until 2017, he worked at the Belle Meade Country Club in Nashville, Tennessee. He is currently a stay-at-home father with his wife, Victoria, and two sons, Harrison and Hampton.

My Memories of Phil...

"THE REHEARSAL SWING"

by

Jon Decker

Former Instructor and Head Instructor

Grand Cypress Academy of Golf (1992-2012)

"...whereas you do not know what will happen tomorrow. For what is your life? It is even a vapor that appears for a little time and then vanishes away." (James 4:14)

I will never forget the moment that changed the course of my life forever. I was a 25-year-old seeking employment and, through the referral of a friend, applied for a bag room position at the Grand Cypress Resort. I was in need of some fast cash, and working in the bag room seemed like a natural fit. As I was being interviewed by human resources, I was asked, "Jon, have you ever considered working at our golf academy?" I responded, "What is the golf academy?" I loved golf and played the game most of my life, but I was unsure what she meant. She replied, "It is our golf school." I responded, "Sure." I was taken via golf cart to the academy to see for myself. When I stepped onto the driving range tee box, I immediately saw a golfing oasis. In front of me were teachers and their students, diligently working on their full swings, while other instructors stood by a practice green, honing their students' short games. It was like I was struck by a bolt of lightning and, for the first time in my life, knew exactly what I wanted to do with my life — I wanted to be a golf instructor.

After being hired to work at the academy, I first had to learn how to pick the driving range. It was not exactly the path I saw for my career after graduating college, but I loved it! I was quickly introduced to the academy staff. The academy was full of talented teachers who would help me develop as a young PGA apprentice and, over time, shape who I am as a man today. The academy was led by our director of instruction, Fred Griffin, recognized as one of the top teachers in the country. Fred regularly worked with PGA TOUR players as well as golfers of all abilities. He oversaw an amazing teaching staff and worked alongside Dr. Ralph Mann, Kathy Whitworth and Phil Rodgers.

When I initially met Phil, he was still competing on the Senior PGA TOUR after playing 17 years on the PGA TOUR. Phil had won six professional events and placed second in the British Open (losing a playoff to Bob Charles in 1963). During the late '80s and early '90s, Phil realized that his playing days were coming to an end, and he began transitioning into full-time teaching. In 1980, his longtime friend Jack Nicklaus called Phil in need of some help with his short game. According to Phil, Nicklaus was hitting fewer greens in regulation and needed to improve his short game to compete. He asked Phil to come to his Florida home for a few days. Phil stayed for two weeks. Every day, Phil worked with Jack on his short game. By the end of August, Nicklaus had not only improved his short game, but he had won the U.S. Open at Baltusrol as well as the PGA Championship at Oak Hill Country Club.

I will admit when I first arrived at Grand Cypress in 1992, I knew very little about Phil Rodgers as a teacher. There was no Golf Channel or social media, so unless your name was Nicklaus,

Watson, Palmer, Norman, Ballesteros, Crenshaw or Kite, you were pretty much just part of the field. The "Tiger effect" was years away, so my knowledge of the golf history of Phil Rodgers and his success did not come through the internet; it came through my co-workers. At the Grand Cypress Academy of Golf, the "King" wasn't Palmer. It was Rodgers.

As I was no longer picking the driving range, my career rapidly advanced to full-time teaching. The first time I taught a golf school with Phil, I was extremely nervous. As I worked my way up the corporate ladder, I observed Phil from afar. Honestly, his delivery to students was different than mine. His commands were more like Sargent Carter's to Gomer Pyle. But deep down, Phil was a big ol' teddy bear. Phil would often pull me aside and give me specific information to teach each student. When I didn't do it right, he would bark at me, "No J.D., do it this way!" Although no one likes to do something the wrong way, I appreciated and gravitated to his teaching style because I knew he cared for me and my development as a golf professional, but most importantly, he cared about his students' improvement.

One day, Phil was teaching putting to a golf school class and mentioned the rehearsal swing to the students. I had never heard that term and, from my limited teaching vocabulary, only used the term "practice swing." I asked Phil one day, "Why do you use the term 'rehearsal swing' with the students?" He barked back to me, "J.D., you're not practicing your technique on the golf course. You're playing the course. You rehearse the shot in the mind first and then allow the body to feel the shot!" He said it with enough conviction to let me know that I better not forget it because it will not only help me as a teacher, but it will also help me as a player. Phil was adamant about all his students rehearsing before every shot, and if you were beating balls with no rehearsal, you were essentially wasting both his and your time.

The rehearsal swing is so important in the short game because these shots are played with so much feel. In the short game, distance control is vital, so every rehearsal swing has a purpose: to gauge the touch needed to make the ball go the correct distance.

The rehearsal swing also allows the player to test the grass and lie. This is so important while hitting shots from the rough. I always stress that rehearsal swings be made at game speed, allowing the player to find the exact swing needed for that shot. There is no exact number of rehearsal swings required in the short game. Prior to hitting the shot, the rehearsal swings should provide a sense of peace, allowing the mind to focus only on the swing needed to make the ball go a certain distance.

I often reflect on my time spent teaching with Phil Rodgers. As the director of instruction at the Medallion Club in Westerville, Ohio, it is now my time to mentor young teachers. I often stress the importance of the rehearsal swing in both the full swing and the short game. In a world of video and launch monitors, it can be difficult to teach "feel" to the average golfer. The rehearsal swing was a game-changer for me both as a player and teacher.

In the game of life, however, there is no physical rehearsal swing. Every day of your life is like every shot on the course — you play them one shot at a time. I look back over my life with my relationships and wish at times that I had a rehearsal swing. Many of my mistakes in relationships have occurred because I have said words out of anger or impatience without thinking. In life, the rehearsal swing needs to be played out in the mind first and with the tongue second.

Over my career, I have spoken to thousands of junior golfers at golf camps, clinics, churches and public schools. In every speech, I have a consistent message: Life is not a dress rehearsal. Life is constantly changing, and each day moves at such a rapid pace. My first day stepping on the tee at Grand Cypress seems like yesterday. I now realize that it is not time to add to my bucket list; it is time to start crossing items off it. Scripture describes life as the dew on the grass that vanishes away with the morning sun. Like the game of golf, life is played one experience at a time. Today is a gift from God; take a moment to thank the Lord for the day and ask Him to lead your steps. This act of prayer is the only rehearsal swing you will get today. After prayer, it is now time to follow God's lead and execute His plan for your day.

On June 26, 2018, Phil Rodgers passed away. The announcement was made through the PGA TOUR, on the Golf Channel and via social media in a beautiful, heartfelt message from Jack and Barbara Nicklaus. I am comforted to know that Phil was a man of faith. In our last conversation over the phone, we talked about our days of teaching golf and reflected on our times at Grand Cypress. Phil knew his time was coming to an end, and I knew it would be the last time we would ever speak. In a very soft-spoken tone, Phil told me that day, "J.D., my mind is still sharp, but my body is failing me." I then asked myself, "What do you say to your mentor, to someone you love and respect and to someone who is getting ready to die?" At that moment, I made a mental rehearsal swing and gave it to the Lord, and He led me to say, "Phil, may I say a prayer with you?" Phil responded, "Yes." I had rehearsed in my mind what I wanted to say to him before we got on the phone, but through the act of asking the Lord for the help I needed, I was able to put my nervousness aside and let my words flow freely. I said a prayer with him and told the man who had done so much for me and my career that I loved him. Like Phil taught me so many years ago, play the shot in your mind first, feel the shot second and then execute it to the best of your ability. Thank you, Phil Rodgers!

Golf Tips Magazine March/April 2022 Issue

Chapter 25

"Five Grooves High, Baby!"

"So, when the woman saw that the tree was good for food, that it was pleasant to the eyes, and a tree desirable to make one wise, she took of its fruit and ate. She also gave to her husband with her, and he ate." (Genesis 3:6)

On a beautiful spring afternoon in the early 2000s, I was hitting balls beside my mentor, Phil Rodgers, as I waited for my next lesson to arrive. Phil had flown up from the Florida Keys to Orlando to teach a golf school for the weekend. During the spring and fall months, Phil would leave his home in San Diego, California, to live in an RV in the Florida Keys to fish, teach golf and enjoy life on the beach. As I was getting ready to hit my next shot, I heard the solid sound of a well-struck iron, followed immediately by a loud, joyful, rough tone, very similar to a drill sergeant barking orders to a private. I heard Phil say, "J.D., that's perfect. That shot was five grooves high, baby!" I turned to Phil in a somewhat confused state and said, "What does five grooves high mean?" He replied, "Dead solid perfect" as he pointed to the center of the clubface and showed me exactly where the ball had been struck. Phil then took his finger and started counting from the bottom of the clubface up toward the top, one groove at a time. Sure enough, the ball mark from his previous shot was exactly in the middle of the fifth groove, in the dead center of the clubface. The irony of the moment was not foreseen when I began my practice session. I was waiting to teach a student, but instead I was receiving a lesson as Phil gave me another one of his many pearls of wisdom. The lesson that day was about club design and the importance of the grooves on the club face.

The grooves on the golf club are designed to create the needed backspin to get the golf ball into the air. The combination of the angle of approach of the downswing, the club's loft and the grooves of the clubface all play a critical role in getting the golf ball airborne. Novice golfers often struggle with this concept of making a divot and allowing the loft and the grooves of the golf club to do the work.

Knowledge is power, so paying attention to where the contact point is on the clubface helps players better understand their golf swing. To illustrate this point during lessons, teachers use launch monitors, apply tape to the face of the club or even spray foot powder on the club face to show the impact point after a student's swing. For illustration purposes, let's look at the bottom groove of any iron and call that groove number one. Any shot hit on groove number one, two or three is going to produce a low shot that struggles to get airborne and, in many cases, rolls along the ground. Players usually refer to this as "hitting the shot thin, low in the face or on the bottom groove." Any shot hit on grooves seven, eight or nine will fly high but weakly through the air because the weight for most irons is toward the bottom of the club, between grooves one and six. Shots hit higher than groove six fly straight but have very little power behind them and usually fall well short of the desired carry distance. This mishit is often described as "hitting it high on the face or scooping it." However, hitting the ball on grooves four, five and six in the center of the clubface is the promised land. Balls hit toward the toe or heel, or off the center of the clubface, will lead to directional issues as well as loss of distance.

"Five grooves high" is also a wonderful way to think about how we as human beings relate to God. We are all human beings that encase a soul. The marriage between body, mind and soul is often tumultuous because the mind and the body, or the "flesh" as it is called in the Scriptures, wants to take from the world. The soul is where God lives in each one of us – if we allow Him to live there – through the act of free will. However, the soul is coveted by the enemy as well. Satan knows that if we reject God in our lives, he can take over the soul. This battle of good versus evil does not start in the soul but in the mind first, and one of the enemies' favorite ploys is deception. In the Garden of Eden, Satan deceived Eve first and Adam second. Prior to Satan's deception, Adam and Eve walked side by side in paradise with God and lived in a world with no sin – in a world that could be described as "five grooves high."

In Christianity, I often think of the clubface and the "five grooves high analogy" as a way of describing my relationship with Jesus Christ. Throughout my lifetime, I have had brief moments where my time with my Lord and Savior seems dead solid perfect or five grooves high. My day is spent in connection with the Lord, and my life seems to fall into place. However, for most of my lifetime, I have often chosen to allow sin into my life and lived at much lower levels as my actions lead me to the bottom grooves of the clubface. When I have chosen to pull away from God, lived on my own and tried to force my way through the day, my life is uncentered. Many of my choices have led to me living on the bottom grooves. Just like a thin golf shot, those days on the lower grooves of life lead to low self-esteem and a poor, defeated attitude. During these times, I often find myself becoming sick or even depressed.

There are also times when I have lived on grooves seven, eight and nine. It is during these moments in my life when I allow pride to take over, and my flesh desires the riches of the world. It is during these prideful times when I have shut God out of my life, replacing Him with the world. What is the world? Bigger homes, nicer cars, lust or more money, just to name a few. Living high on the clubface leads to a false sense of security. Many of the riches of the world are necessary, like shelter, transportation and money. These worldly items themselves are not sin. The sin occurs when we, as human beings, create a false idol with our material possessions and replace God with our false idols. Like a golf shot hit very high on the clubface, when I have lived on the higher grooves of life, I come up short and feel an emptiness in my life.

However, there is good news! Jesus died for our sins, and belief in Him will ultimately lead us, one day at a time, from the fairways of this lifetime to the perfect place: Heaven. According to the Scriptures, Heaven is a place that never operates at a lower level or higher level by earthly standards but at a level of God's perfection. When I heard that Phil had left this world to begin his everlasting life, my mind was flooded with all the memories of the time we had spent together along with my fellow instructors at Grand Cypress. In my mind, I could see him in Heaven and hear his loud, joyful voice proclaiming to me, "J.D., the promised land is dead solid perfect! It's five grooves high, baby!"

Golf Tips Magazine Nov/Dec 2023 Issue

My last photo with Phil. (Left to right): Todd Meena, Will Roberts, Blake Terry, Phil Rodgers, Jon Decker and Gus Holbrook.

CHAPTER 26

READY! ONE, TWO, SWING, SWING

"But, beloved, do not forget this one thing that with the Lord one day is as a thousand years, and a thousand years as one day." (2 Peter 3:8)

As a young apprentice in my mid-20s, I vividly remember cutting my teeth in the golf business during Phil Rodger's short game school as a teaching assistant. I started working at the Grand Cypress Academy of Golf in 1992 and was very green in my knowledge of golf instruction. My job responsibilities included setting up the golf schools as well as assisting the students during their three-day short game boot camp. Phil's schools were always well-attended, usually between 12 and 16 students, and all the students were eager to receive some of his short game magic. The short game school included chipping, pitching, bunker and putting along with trouble shots and on-course instruction.

I remember the first presentation I heard Phil deliver on putting. Phil talked about the timing of the putting stroke and showed the students the research and data accumulated by Dr. Ralph Mann. Dr. Mann filmed the top PGA TOUR players with high-speed video hitting 4-, 8-, 16- and 32-foot putts. The video not only recorded their setup, length of backswing and follow through, but it also timed their putting strokes. This is when I had my first of many "aha" moments listening to Phil's presentations.

Phil talked about the time of the stroke from the beginning of the stroke, just as the putter started back, as well as the time of the downswing (the time from the end of the backswing to the golf ball). Just like a child swinging on a swing set, the downswing was twice as fast as the backswing. Once the player strikes the golf ball with the putter, the putter naturally slows down through friction, as long as the player allows gravity to accelerate the putter and resist the temptation to add force. No matter what length the TOUR players faced — 4, 8,16 or 32 feet — their time back and to the golf ball with the putter was virtually the same, to the hundredth of a second. That time was the constant; the variables were the different length of strokes needed to make the ball go different distances. Obviously a 32-foot putt will have a longer swing back and through than a 4-foot putt, but the time back and to the ball for the TOUR players was constant: one second.

To emphasis his point, Phil had all the students stand in the middle of the green with four or five golf balls about 30 feet from the fringe of the green. He then had the students putt the ball to the fringe, not the hole, so that all their focus was on the speed of the greens and distance control. Like the conductor of a philharmonic orchestra standing on a raised podium, Phil would then yell out to the students, "Ready, one, two, swing, swing." The "ready" was like the conductor tapping his baton on the music stand to get the orchestra's attention. The "one, two" were to get the students' count on the conductor's cadence, and the "swing, swing" was the physical act of swinging the putter back and through. After five minutes, all of the golf school students were swinging their putters at the same time and, for the most part, at the same tempo as a PGA TOUR player. I stood at the edge of the green and watched in amazement as all the students' golf balls rolled at the same time and speed to the edge of the green, often from students who had come to the school with handicaps much higher than my age.

As soon as the school was over and my duties of cleaning up the golf school were finished, I raced to my car, got my putter and headed straight for the putting green. I put three balls in the center of the green, counted in my head, "Ready, one, two, swing, swing," and hit my first putt. My golf ball came up well short of the fringe. I tried again and again, but each time my ball came up short. I left the putting green and thought to myself, "This doesn't work." I quickly surmised in my limited understanding of the complexities of teaching the game of golf that this exercise was for beginners and was not needed by me.

The next day, Phil was teaching another golf school, and I listened to his putting presentation again, trying to figure out why this method was working for the students and not for me. I suddenly realized that Phil's cadence counting was faster than my cadence. I always joked with Phil, "I'm from the South, Phil, I talk slower than Californians." During his golf school, Phil was not only the conductor, but he was also the metronome, setting the pace for the swing for his students to follow. After 20 years of teaching at Grand Cypress, I realized that what matters most in counting "one, two, swing, swing" was not the verbal words, but the cadence of the count in between the words. In other words, timing is everything.

In my spiritual life, my conductor is Jesus Christ. Looking back at my life, I have too often made the mistake of looking ahead, rushing through life with eagerness toward future events, like a child counting down the days to Christmas morning. I have also had dark periods of my life and felt stuck, often looking back and holding onto bad memories, bad relationships or mistakes like they were a badge of honor. I now understand that God wants to share my daily walk together. He does not want me living in the past or living in the future, but living with me where I am at that moment, one second at a time. In other words, God wants me to live in the moment where my shoes are planted that day. I am convinced this life skill is the difference between the PGA TOUR player who wins the weekly tournament and the one who misses the cut. Winning each week on TOUR has less to do with the physical skills of the players and more to do with their mental approach during the week.

Allowing God to be the conductor and metronome for my life and trusting His cadence for my life takes discipline. Starting the day out first with the Lord through prayer, reading scripture, devotionals and meditation is now the most important part of my day. Just like Phil saying to his pupils, "Ready," to let his students know his count is about to begin, when I go to the Lord first to begin each day, I am acknowledging to the Father that I am ready to follow His lead. God then uses the Holy Spirit as my own personal metronome. His count sets my personal cadence, giving me the peace, wisdom and guidance needed for that day. On days when my count is off, and it often is, I pray for His cadence to get me back on track.

My time on this Earth is coming to an end very, very soon. As a grown man now in his 50s, I realize that I have little time left before I die. I came into this world on January 12, 1967, in Augusta, Georgia. That day of my life is when God gave me my first breath and spoke to my life's journey and said, "Ready." At some point soon, at a time and place that only He knows, I will take my last breath. Like Phil proclaiming, "One, two, swing, swing," to his students, I now realize the quality time spent between that first and last breath is what matters most.

Although, by earthly standards, I may have another 20, 30, 40 or, who knows, 50 years left, by God's standard of time, I have only seconds. As the scripture says, one day to God is like a thousand years to His beloved. This means from God's perspective, my time left on this planet is a mere second, before I return home to Him. Like the "one, two, swing, swing" of life, I now try to spend what time I have left more with God and those I love and less with the world. Tomorrow is promised to no one, so get in tune with the conductor, follow His count and watch Him lead the flow of your life to the fringes of Heaven, one shot at a time...

Golf Tips Magazine July/August Issue 2024

Epilogue: Somewhere In Between

"Then two robbers were crucified with Him, one on the right and another on the left." (Matthew 27:38)

"Assuredly, I say to you, today you will be with Me in Paradise." (Luke 23:43)

One of the biggest complaints I hear from my students is, "I can hit the ball great on the driving range but can't take it to the course." I too know this feeling and share in my students' pain. I break teaching down into three distinct levels. Level one is learning to hit the ball on the driving range and in the short-game areas. I tell my students, "If you can't do it here on the range, it will not happen on the course." Level two is learning to take what you have learned on the driving range and apply it to the golf course. This level requires that a student practice and perfect a pre-shot routine and play every shot toward a single target, no matter the distance. Level three is learning how to perform under pressure. Pressure for most of my students is playing in the member/guest tournament or being able to tee off while others are watching. All three levels require practice and repetition and take years to perfect. But, after a lifetime of playing and teaching this game, I find that most of my students' struggles occur not at levels one, two or three but somewhere in between.

For example, after a few lessons, most of my students are ready to take their game to the course. However, when they arrive at the first tee, they are not thinking about what side of the tee box to set up on, or which way the wind is blowing or their target; they are thinking about their golf swing. They are somewhere in between level one and level two. For many of my tournament players, they struggle when they get under pressure during a member/guest, high school tryouts or trying to qualify for the

U.S. Open. They are put into an uncomfortable situation for the first time and are not used to their heart rate increasing, shortness of breath and the feeling that their golf swing feels as though they are having an out-of-body experience. Gone is the comfort of their familiar foursome they always play with on the weekends. They are somewhere in between level two and level three. I have found that living somewhere in between levels applies to my life and faith journey as well.

After my divorce, I experienced some financial hardships, and I was forced to live with friends, family and basically out of a suitcase for years. I had gone from living in a lakefront home to homeless, and without God, my family and my friends, I would have never made it. I learned to thank God every day for the blessings of others and what they were providing for me during my time of need. I will forever be grateful for all of the people who helped me during those lean years. Although I wasn't living in a lakefront home, I also wasn't out on a cold street, scraping trash cans for food. I was somewhere in between.

I believe in Heaven, and I also believe in Hell, and I believe Earth is simply somewhere in between. We live in a fallen world and are asked by God to spread His light. More than 2,000 years ago, on a skull-shaped hilltop in Jerusalem known as Golgotha, or Calvary, three men were crucified. On one side was a thief, who sided with the world as he hung on the cross, mocking Jesus. On the other end was another thief, who saw the errors of his ways and spoke these final words to Jesus: ***"Remember me when you come into Your kingdom" (Luke 23:42)***. And somewhere in between those two thieves hung the Son of God, Jesus Christ.

I will never be able to live up to God's standard, a standard that is laid out in the Bible and Ten Commandments. I look at my life and what I have done with it, and then I look at God's standard. I know that my attempts have fallen short, but I am comforted knowing that my Savior is somewhere in between.

For years, God used my nomadic lifestyle to prepare me for the writing of this book. God had my full attention, and for the first time in my life, I followed His lead one day at a time. During this time, I also grew a soft spot in my heart for the homeless and those in need. I began praying to God each time I saw a homeless person, knowing that person could be me if it were not for the love and support of my family.

In 2018, I pulled up to a stop light and saw a homeless man. He was tired and dirty and looked as though everything he owned was in a trash bag lying by his feet. I gave him my change, told him "God bless" and drove away. As I pulled off, God suddenly downloaded a poem to me. I hurried home and wrote the poem but had no idea why God gave it to me and what I was supposed to do with it. I now realize that the poem God first gave me for this book, ironically, would be the last words of the book. Over time, the rest of the words for the book were simply somewhere in between.

Somewhere in Between…

Cruising to the red light, I caught a glimpse of a man holding a cardboard sign.

His face revealed a life, I'm sure, that was quite different than mine.

Our eyes never met, but I'm willing to bet, he saw me from afar.

The light glaring red, guilt riding shotgun. Where's the change I keep in the car?

Our eyes now meet, the transaction complete and I sped away to pray.

Thank God for the warm bed, where I lay my head, to sleep my problems away.

I struggle with my current state, my destination, comparing my life to the Joneses down the street.

While the homeless carry their lives on their shoulders, that are transported by two weary feet.

Father, I am not rich nor am I poor, and there's places I've never seen.

I live no life of luxury, but I'm grateful, thankful, and content, living life somewhere in between…

Golf Tips Magazine Sept/Oct 2024 Issue

ABOUT THE AUTHOR

Jon Decker is currently the director of instruction for The Medallion Club in Westerville, Ohio and works seasonally at the Wyndemere Country Club in Naples, Florida (December-March). He has been a PGA member since May of 1997. He is the senior editor and *Top 25 Instructor* for *Golf Tips Magazine* where he writes instructional articles, produces instructional videos as well as writes his Christian golf feature, *Fairways to Heaven.* He previously was director of instruction at the New Albany Country Club in New Albany, Ohio. Prior to working in Ohio, Jon was a head instructor at the Grand Cypress Academy of Golf in Orlando, Florida where he worked twenty years under Top 100 Teachers Fred Griffin and Phil Rodgers. In 2016, Jon published his first book, *Golf is My Life: Glorifying God Through the Game.* In 2015, Jon was named the *Southern Ohio Teacher of the Year.* Jon has taught players of all levels, including players on the PGA Tour, LPGA Tour, Champions Tour. He has coached at the PGA Championship (2011-2014) and the Women's U.S. Open in 2007.

Follow Jon on his website DeckerGolf.com

Facebook, Instagram, YouTube or LinkedIn

ABOUT THE EDITOR

Bill Studenc, who began working in journalism and communications at *The Mountaineer* newspaper in Waynesville, North Carolina, in 1983, retired in January 2021 as chief communications officer at Western Carolina University after a career spanning more than 32 years. He earned his bachelor's degree in journalism and history at the University of North Carolina-Chapel Hill and his master's degree in public affairs at WCU. He has been editor of *The News Record* of Madison County and a contributor to the *Asheville Citizen-Times*, *Out 'n' About*, *Smoky Mountain Living* magazine and the *Black Mountain News*, all in North Carolina. He writes a regular column for *The Mountaineer* and provides writing and editing services to clients including WCU, Florida Gulf Coast University, Ohio University, Lake Junaluska Conference and Retreat Center and Buris Chalmers Creative. Bill grew up in Black Mountain, North Carolina, where his brother Scott was an Owen High School classmate of author Jon Decker.

Go to DeckerGolf.com to order Jon's first book, *Golf Is My Life: Glorifying God Through the Game.*

Subscribe to Golf Tips Magazine for more of Jon's Fairways To Heaven and golf instructional articles.

Speaking engagements and online instruction available through DeckerGolf.com

www.ingramcontent.com/pod-product-compliance
Lightning Source LLC
Chambersburg PA
CBHW021437150726
47989CB00001B/275